HARVESTING PHOTONS

A PHOTOGRAPHIC VOYAGE THROUGH THE AMERICAN WEST

William J Wood Jr

Copyright © 2017

No part of this book may be reproduced in any form, or by any electronic, mechanical, or other means, without permission in writing from the author or publisher.

All photography by William J Wood Jr

copyright © 2017

Cover photo:

Mesquite Flats Sand Dunes,

Death Valley National Park

For

My Fellow Travelers and Hosts

Travelers

Barbara O. Ward-Wood

Waffles

Photons Bus, home on the road

Hosts

John Wood, Stockton

Robert G. Robb, Phoenix

Anne Wood, Tucson

Steve Villaescuza, Gnomanium

Richard Rubinstein, Santa Fe

Table of Contents
Introduction
Chapter 1. Planning Escape
Chapter 2. The Balm of Preparation
Chapter 3. Stockton to Palm Springs
Chapter 4. Palm Springs to Phoenix
Chapter 5. Homeward Bound
Chapter 6. Tin Cup and the Sonoran Desert
Chapter 7. Santa Fe-Half the Way
Chapter 8. Georgia Okeeffe's Art is not Vaginal
Chapter 9. Los Alamos: Beautiful Town, Ugly Bomb
Chapter 10. Goodbye Santa Fe
Chapter 11. Painted and Petrified
Chapter 12. Utah or Death (Valley)
Chapter 13. Death Valley Daze and the Harvest of Photons
Chapter 14. Ghosts and UFOs
Chapter 15. Wrong Turn, Right Move
Chapter 16. Well Oiled Machine
Chapter 17. To Morro Bay Today
Chapter 18. Half Moon Bay, Full Wind Night
Chapter 19. Requiem for a Voyage
Chapter 20. The RV Industry is Booming
Chapter 21. RV Construction for Idiots
Chapter 22. How Not to Purchase an RV
Chapter 23. Can RVs Ever Be Green?
About the Author
Other Books by William J Wood Jr

Introduction

Two weeks before Christmas, my wife and I left Portland, Oregon, in the rain, heading south in our new Class A Recreational Vehicle, a Coachman Pursuit 31SB. I had dreamed of owning a big Class A, riding the roads high above the traffic, watching the world float by through a huge shiny windshield. Now I had my dream coach.

This wasn't a casual vacation. It was an escape. I sought escape. Empowered bureaucrats terminated my privileges at the medical center where I had practiced for thirty years. After years of challenging education, rigorous surgical training and thirty years of busy practice, I couldn't agree with management's policy of keeping my mouth shut whenever I encountered poor or devious behavior. No amount of leadership training made me believe I had given up the traditional authority of a physician.

I was weary. Surgery is a stressful profession, made more stressful in recent years by insipid Soviet-style bureaucracy imposed on the medical profession by corporate glad handers in shiny suits. The soft talking, secretive business school graduates, now the masters of the healthcare universe, long ago fled the redolent hospital corridors for more manicured digs in office buildings with city views and grease-boarded conference rooms.

From towers, they designed self-congratulatory paradigms and spread fear of liability and stuffed their pockets with profit. None of these plantation overseers knew anything about medicine, except for a few conscripted doctor-administrators, suffering from Stockholm Syndrome. They never treated a patient or witnessed suffering or answered phone calls in the middle of the night.

The masters glibly sang the corporate lingo, preferring the term, workforce, to describe the doctors, nurses and employees that provided the actual labor of healthcare. Doctor morphed into provider; patients were insured lives. Stern speeches about mission and zero tolerance oozed executive proclamation.

Run, doctors, run!

Barb and I would join the families in Tucson at Mom's house for Christmas. My son, Joshua, and his girlfriend, on break from college in Eugene, Oregon, would fly down. We would stay a few days in Stockton at my brother's house in a pleasant, leafy neighborhood that backed up to the California Delta, one-thousand miles of waterway that one could sail on to San Francisco or Napa, if one had plenty of time. It would be golf weather in Arizona, months before golf weather returned to Portland. Escape.

Barb and I bought a Coleman tent trailer when we were first married. We towed it behind my Toyota FJ40 Land Cruiser, the original FJ, box-shaped with all-metal interior and jump seats, a fearsome off-road vehicle. I wish I had kept the FJ. The originals are a coveted cult vehicle among off-road enthusiasts. I forget what I sold it for, but refurbished models now sell for forty thousand and up.

In 1985, we moved to Houston, towing our Coleman. I did a fellowship in Surgical Oncology at MD Anderson Medical Center. We moved to Portland where we entered our medical practices, Barb as an Internal Medicine MD. Before we left Houston, I sold the Coleman trailer and the FJ40 and bought a Volkswagen Westfalia camper van.

The Westfalia took us cross-country, in comfort, with our dogs. There was a large luggage well in back, perfect for our dogs, Biscuit, a Chesapeake mix, and Chevis, a ruddy red Golden Retriever. The mid-section had a huge floor space in front of a long bench seat. The dining table hinged out and there was a dorm-room-size refrigerator. You could stand up inside after popping the roof.

I remember watching thousands of mosquitoes dance behind the mesh screen at Jackson Hole. Unlike the tent trailer, in the Westfalia you had the luxury of a room and a couch as you drove. Set up for camp was a blink, just pop the top. The only downside of the Westfalia was the underpowered engine, a 1.9 L, 4 cylinder, 76-hp tail dragger that needed second gear for even moderate hills.

In Oregon, I sold the Westfalia and bought a Toyota 4-Runner, a much better vehicle for exploring the backcountry. Years later I ran into the friend who had bought the Westfalia. He let me drive it. Letting out the clutch, I remembered that feeble engine that could barely overcome inertia. I had erased that memory.

The Westfalia was a Class B. Class Bs are vans with custom construction. Our first motorhome, a Class C Coachman Catalina, had a bunk bed extending over the top of the cab. The C designation comes from word cabover. A 365-horsepower, 6.8 L gas Triton V-10 engine easily powered the comfortable camper. The Triton V-10 will run on only 5 cylinders as a fail-safe measure if it detects a rise in operating temperature.

My family of three enjoyed several RV vacations in the Catalina. We camped in Yellowstone on our way to visit friends in Craig, Colorado. Our tour of the Sierra Nevada included camps at Yosemite, Sequoia, Las Vegas and Mono Lake. Vancouver Island was the best trip, with a fishing charter off Port Hardy that netted two hundred pounds of Chinook and Coho salmon and halibut.

The Catalina had no slide outs and no bedroom. Barb and Joshua slept in the cabover bunk and I the jack-knife couch. Teenagers don't wake up first thing in the morning, so we would haul Joshua's sleeping body off the cabover onto the couch, belt him in, and head down the road in the wee hours, logging several hundred miles before he regained consciousness.

We discovered other uses for the Catalina. We took it on Boy Scout trips. The boys competed to see who got to ride in the Party Bus. In his teen years, Joshua and friends discovered the RV was the perfect place for all night non-sleepovers, where loud voices would not disturb sleeping parents.

The era of family trips faded. I took a group of friends in the Catalina to Montana for a memorial service. After, we had a great backpack into the Lee Metcalf Wilderness.

Coming back from photographing the blood moon on Paulina Peak in central Oregon, the Catalina stalled out at a traffic light. It had developed a leak in the cooling line from the transmission. The transmission was toast. My mechanic rebuilt the transmission and put in a heavy-duty torque converter. At the end of its days, the Catalina rested, like the ghost of Robert E. Lee, in the shade of our pin oaks, growing moss and singing Oh Lonesome Me.

I began backpacking with old friends from my Arizona days. After graduating from the University of Arizona, our family-like circle had dispersed to pursue careers. Our good friend, Canoe, after cofounding the Buffalo Gap chain stores in Tucson, had moved to Bozeman, Montana where she ran a similar recycling business called the Catwalk. Her real name was Cathy. We all had nicknames back then. Mine was The Gnome. Canoe spawned the idea of getting everyone together in Montana.

Canoe knew Yellowstone like the back of her hand. She organized the reunion that involved many emails, calls and frustrations trying to get everyone together. Not having hoisted a backpack in years, we worried about our trail hardiness. Canoe took the brunt of the whining and vented her frustration with the comment, "What is this, the Geezer Geyser tour?" The name stuck in shortened form and we became the Geezers. Over time, the Geezer email list grew to thirty-six names.

The Yellowstone trip had magic. Twelve Geezers trekked into the Lamar Valley and camped at Cache Creek, below the den of the Druid wolf pack. We felt young again. We acted young, singing, pulling pranks and laughing the unhindered pure laughter of youth.

After this inaugural trip, it was easier to corral the Geezers. We went on many excellent adventures. We explored the Escalante River in Utah, the San Juan Mountains in Colorado, and in Arizona, the state we knew well, the Chiricahua Mountains, the Galiuro Mountains, the Pinaleno Mountains and the Superstitions.

There were losses along the way. Jay, my best friend from high school and an avid soccer player, passed without warning. Canoe developed major complications from treatment of an autoimmune disorder and spent her last brave and noble days in Tennessee with her sisters. Walter, a Yellowstone Geezer, died suddenly at home. We scattered ashes in beautiful places. Don't rest; continue to explore this bright world. Nothing induces a sense of mortality better than death.

During the frustrating years at the end of my practice, I engaged in an activity my grandmother called wishbooking. That was her word when she caught my father, or his siblings, leafing through Montgomery Ward catalogues. It was the Depression years then and it did no good to wander through pages of thick catalogues of merchandise the family could not afford. She caught me wishbooking a few times. But Grandmother Laverne Tennessee Nobles Wood, bless her loving heart and encompassing hugs, was long gone. I could wishbook with only an echo of guilt.

When I could enjoy unstressed time at home, I wishbooked on the RV Trader website. I viewed hundreds of new and used RVs for sale within 50 miles, 100 miles, 250 miles or, heck, nationwide. During the long, wet, grey Oregon winters I hallucinated road trips through mountains and deserts, a sun-bright diorama through a cinema-wide windshield, floating high above the rushing pulse of dashed lines into a concrete infinity. Thus therapy.

I took up photography. Worshiping Ansel Adams, I saw myself photographing western skies. I could develop the images in my mobile road home. The dream of the Class A rig was a dream of escape. I wanted to escape the stress of running a practice and caring for patients, something I took seriously, in a medical system that treated physicians like Walmart employees. No offense to actual Walmart employees. After thirty years in Oregon, I wanted to escape winter. My wishbooking was a manifestation, or a symptom, of a desire to escape, sane or not.

Geezers in Montana

The Catalina at Crater Lake, Oregon

CHAPTER 1

PLANNING ESCAPE

At the end of my surgery career my colleagues on the medical staff committee at my hospital decided I had accumulated too many complaints and sought to terminate my hospital privileges. I was a very amiable and humorous doctor, but on rare occasions I ran into poor behavior from nurses or employees or colleagues and I have always believed I had earned the authority, as a senior surgeon with thirty years of service, to communicate disapproval.

The corporate administrators have been on a mission, for years, to bring down the traditional authority of physicians. As the system accumulated employed doctors, the tone of administrators changed from one of collegiality to one of disdain.

A phrase I heard often in the locker room was: "You have to be very careful what you say to the nurses now days." Why, I would think. What a horrible atmosphere! Medical care is difficult enough without having to walk around constantly fearful of what you say to others.

The suit-wearing boys no longer wanted to have doctors in charge of the health care team. Why should they? The corporation employed the doctors. It collected the premiums and so, held the money. The system owned the doctors and the patients and the facilities, sort of like a monopoly, I believe is the term.

Doctors could no longer intimidate administrators by threatening to "take their patients elsewhere," since the doctors no longer had patients. Patients were customers of the healthcare and insurance monopoly. The executives wanted as much control as possible over their workforce. They wanted quotas, practice protocols, aggressive credentialing and dictatorial control over annoying issues like cooperation with regulatory mandates, billing, risk management (especially institutional risk) and strict adherence to bureaucratic-style behavior codes.

Nurses and employees got the message. Any criticism coming from a doctor was negated by filing a complaint against said doctor. Someone called it, first complaint wins. Despite my honest and accurate descriptions of some truly outrageous and even lethal behaviors coming from some of those who had complained about me, my moralistic colleagues never once agreed with my point of view.

We few remaining private practice doctors were easy targets. We were naked among those royally blessed by management, the employed groups. Those who passed judgment on me at my trial were employed minions who knew who buttered their bread. I sensed it bothered them that I didn't project much anxiety. I was at the end of my career either way. I had enough savings to retire. It was all a matter of pride.

As my slow crucifixion progressed, I mused what to do next. I dreamed of touring beautiful places in the comfort of a home-like bus. The Coachman Pursuit 31SB, a new model, was offered by several dealers on RV Trader, the closest in Davis, California. The floor plan was perfect, and the price far less than what I expected to pay for a new Class A.

When I told Barb my idea of getting a new RV, she, expectedly, told me we shouldn't be spending money right before we retired. I considered that, and then I called the dealer in Sacramento. John, my brother, lived in nearby Stockton, so I could stay with him and hit the golf course as a bonus.

The faithful Coachman Catalina took me on a last voyage, leaving home at four am and arriving at five pm at John's, six hundred twenty-seven miles. I discovered the microwave was not working. Just before I traded it in, I heard an unfamiliar high-pitched whine during acceleration, but it had good power and drove fine. At the dealer's, a guy in work clothes looked over the exterior and stomped on the roof. He said, gruffly, "This needs some work."

I had agreed, after several phone conversations with the salesman, Eric, on a trade-in price of $10,000 for the Catalina, which I considered fair since the NADA price quote was $16,000. Plus I was buying the Pursuit with no haggling. I had talked several times to Eric at the Davis office and discussed his father's fight with cancer.

There was a different salesman at the Sacramento office. He told me the Catalina needed a new roof. He wasn't happy with the trade-in price. I told him I had just driven six hundred miles to do this deal and had been completely honest with all the questions coming from Eric, including sending many pictures. I told him there was no evidence of a roof leak and pointed out that the vehicle stayed outside in Oregon where it rained all the time, so I would have known. I also showed him ads for identical models of the same vintage on RV Trader. He did the usual sales maneuver of talking to his boss. He returned and told me he was doing me a special favor to let the deal go through.

I expected the thirty-one-foot Pursuit wouldn't look much larger than my twenty-two-foot Catalina. When I saw it for the first time, I thought they had the wrong vehicle. It looked massive compared to the Catalina. I felt disoriented in the driver's seat, with no innate sense of the boundaries of the vehicle that extended forever in the rear-view mirror. There was no offer of a tutorial or a practice drive. When I drove out the lot, it was like plunging into ice water.

To avoid paying California sales tax I had to drive the Pursuit to Reno, Nevada and take legal possession there. OK. An affably grizzled guy walked up, introduced himself as Rocky, and told me to follow him in his pickup. He gave me a brief description of the route to Reno.

I followed Rocky's pickup up I-80 through the curves of Donner Pass into Reno. Rocky was in a hurry. When I smelled his cheerful breath at the UPS in Reno, I realized he had started his evening libations early. Through the pass, I thought I was tipping over on the curves, staring down the steep plunge to Donner Lake. I was sweating and nauseous. I was rocky.

The drive back to Stockton was better since I controlled my own preferred speed sans Rocky, but I hit rush hour in Sacramento. I constantly worried I was crowding other vehicles or drifting out of my lane. As I gained time behind the wheel, I became more comfortable driving the big rig. One mental technique that helped in busy city driving was to imagine driving a sports car. The Triton V-10 had adequate power to zip across crowded lanes or merge on entrance ramps.

At John's house, feeling frazzled, I joined Rocky with a bourbon on the rocks. John and his wife, Peggy, were impressed with the new RV. It was bigger and roomier than the old Catalina. I offered to let John drive it. He declined. He said, "I don't see how you can drive this thing." My thought was that I had paid for it so I better learn how to drive it.

I left early from Stockton to get through Sacramento before rush hour on I-5. With time, I became more comfortable in the driver's seat. I fidgeted for many miles with the seat position. Somewhere before Redding, in the last northern gasp of California's great Central Valley, the sun came up. The fresh green fields on each side of the road were glowing in golden light with bright orange poppies and a delicate mist draping the distant rolling hills. Here was my wishbooking vision born from a dark Oregon winter come to life, Oz-like, in vivid color. I don't know how many epiphanies we get in this life, but I cashed one in on that sunrise. That's all I have to say about that.

I grew up in Texas and Arizona. After thirty years in Oregon I have never adapted to the sunless marine-layer wintertide. My mood varies in direct proportion to the intensity of sunlight.

Just now, as I write this, the sun has come out and my mood lightens.

One day, when Joshua was five, it was raining and he was entertaining himself by running in circles in the rain. I said, "Don't you want to move to Arizona where your Dad is from?" He said, with precocious intelligence and not bothering to stop his circles, "You forget, Dad. I grew up here."

The new Pursuit 31SB, heading home to Oregon

Chapter 2

The Balm of Preparation

The corporate stone of apoplexy sealed my crypt. I lost my Fair Hearing at the hospital. I requested only to resign with dignity after my dedicated years of service. The corporate lawyer was not interested in compromise. Compromise was fear of liability and his job was to quash all risk of liability.

The Medical Staff Bylaws outlined the Fair Hearing Procedure, inscribed in ponderous legalese years ago after a trial in Oregon struck fear into hospital administrators. The medical staff of a small hospital on the Oregon coast terminated a surgeon, Dr. Timothy Patrick, for alleged substandard practices. Those staff members conducting the peer review were members of a large clinic that Dr. Patrick had declined to join and were, therefore, economic competitors. Dr. Patrick sued on the basis of antitrust violation and won $2.2 million in damages. The United States Court of Appeals for the Ninth Circuit overturned the verdict, but the United States Supreme Court (Patrick v. Burget, 1988) upheld.

I chaired the Quality Assurance Committee at the hospital around the time of the Patrick case. Administrative members of the Committee frequently invoked the Patrick case as a rationale for not pursuing certain issues too vigorously. Now the fortified bylaws that emerged from that paranoia were being used against me.

My lawyer warned me that the Fair Hearing was a nasty kangaroo court. It was. The corporate attorney selected a judge and a panel of three physicians. After sitting for several hours, listening to an intensely biased character assassination, I presented my side of the complaints. I admitted that two of the nine complaints were legitimate and that I had lost my temper and had spoken harshly. I pointed out that I personally apologized to these individuals, one of whom gave me a hug and told me I was "sweet."

The other seven complaints, I argued, described poor behaviors from the complainants themselves and I had rightly criticized them within my authority as the physician of the patient. The physicians on the panel nodded their heads at me as I described these incidents. However, at the closing argument, the prosecuting attorney instructed the panel that their job was not to judge the fairness of the complaints, but was only and narrowly to judge whether the Medical Staff adhered to the correct procedures as outlined in the bylaws. In that context, Goliath wins and David must sit in the corner.

I could have appealed, but I was heartsick and ready to leave. My patients, who always gave me warm, genuine feedback with a big hug at the last visit, were astonished. They recognized my dedication to their care and my honesty. These measures of quality mean little any more inside the corporate bubble.

I wrote a rebuttal to the Fair Hearing report and insisted it be placed in my medical staff file. The entire process left me nauseated at an existential level. I closed my practice a few months sooner than I would have anyway and made preparations to head south in the new RV and make it to Tucson by Christmas.

Barb, a meticulous organizer, stocked the RV with most of the things we would need. I made a list of things I wanted to have, including golf clubs, photography equipment, my guitar, computers, fly-fishing gear, hiking gear and a good size collection of DVD movies. All these favorite things would not have fit into the old Catalina.

We planned to head east on I-84 and swing down through Salt Lake and into southern Utah. For years, I had wanted to explore Canyonlands. There were several RV parks on the perimeter. As the date of departure drew near, I checked the weather and road conditions. A big storm blew in from the Pacific. Interstate 84 in the Columbia Gorge had black ice. The webcams showed snow and ice in Idaho. Salt Lake was raining, but I didn't want to risk traveling with my new RV over several hundred miles of frozen macadam.

We decided to avoid the snow and took I-5 through California that had two potential trouble spots: Siskiyou Pass south of Ashland and Shasta Pass in California. Both had only light snow. We left our house in the hands of two of Joshua's good friends, whom we knew and trusted. They were excited about living on their own, as was Joshua, who would join them for Christmas break.

The emotional damage of my battle with my medical staff caused me not to experience the anticipatory excitement that always overcame me when preparing for a voyage. Before any long trip, I research. Before Peru, Africa, Cambodia, Europe, Greece and other destinations I read many travel books and other pertinent literature to prepare. Now, my usual drive to discover new worlds was in a closet ranting about Kafka. I decided the only goal was Tucson by Christmas and everything else would work out as we traveled.

We left on December 12 at 4:00 am and drove straight through to my brother's house in Stockton. There was an hour delay at a truck stop in southern Oregon. We couldn't find our cat, Waffles. I thought she might have run out the door when I went to fill the gas. We searched on foot for almost an hour and then drove around the area. Suddenly, our silent, magical friend was on the floor between our seats. She had found a secret hiding place in the RV. Later we would discover her secret spot.

Chapter 3

Stockton to Palm Springs
Where did Waffles go?

A big storm rolled in the day we left Stockton, bound for Palm Springs. We didn't want to battle Los Angeles traffic so we plotted to exit I-5 for the 138, then run south on the 14 through Palmdale, hook up with I-15 into San Bernardino, then merge into I-10 into Palm Springs. I made reservations at The Emerald Desert RV Resort in Palm Desert, which would be the most expensive RV park of the trip.

I've never been a fan of wind. I hadn't yet driven the new Pursuit through big winds. Years ago, we experienced nerve-wracking winds in the Catalina driving across Wyoming. In my experience, one always experiences an Aeolian welcome in Wyoming. I drove my motorcycle, a full-fairing BMW R90, at a thirty-degree angle through the state. The old saying is: "The wind doesn't blow in Wyoming, it sucks."

Rain and wind started at Manteca, south of Stockton, and stayed with us all the way to Palm Springs. Gusts shoved us into the emergency lane, but I learned to keep position with constant small pressure on the steering wheel. Driving a bus-size vehicle required a different technique than zoning out in a sedan or a truck. The big boy constantly wandered to either side. After a while, steering micro-corrections became subconscious and I could maintain my lane position. I discovered when passing a large tractor-trailer to expect a sudden lateral push from the bow wave coming off the truck cab.

After Palmdale, we pulled into an abandoned gas station

for a break. For the second time Waffles vanished. I tend to panic when my pet is lost. We looked for possible hiding places. Then we heard her meowing under the bed that attached to a plywood box that had, maybe, an inch and a half gap between the bed frame and the box. I couldn't imagine her squeezing through that narrow slot. No here-kitty cooing was making her squeeze out. We tried to coax her into a drawer. She no buy that. She contentedly explored her new cave. We put food into the drawer. No thanks, meow, meow. Everyone knows you can't teach a cat tricks. I admire the species for their independent nature, but I didn't want Waffles to starve independently. You can't eat a name.

    Back on the road, I planned to hit the next Home Depot and buy a circular saw to cut a hole in the plywood. Then, as before, she appeared, ironically, behind the doghouse, the hump between the driver and passenger that covers the engine. We never discovered how she had gotten under the bed and she never went there again.

    We discovered something else after nightfall. The low beams were atrocious. The feeble cone of visibility from the LED headlights extinguished sharply thirty yards ahead. I had no time for reaction when objects popped out of the darkness. I hit the high beam every chance I got, but often there was a line of oncoming cars in the single-lane going over Cajon Junction and I didn't want to blind everyone.

    I-10 welcomed us with a torrential rainstorm and California rush-hour traffic. When we exited and took a left on Gerald Ford Drive, a centrist himself, my neck had hot needles and my speech was more incoherent than usual. We turned on Frank Sinatra Drive, silent now after a great career, and pulled up to the gate of the Emerald Desert RV Resort.

    The gates were not the emerald gates of Oz. They were locked. We had been warned. The woman had told us to look in the mail slot in the office for our pass code and information. I perceived what appeared to be an office on the other side. I scaled the gate and entered the small structure. There were no mail slots. Barb scaled the gate, disappeared into the dark, and came back several minutes later with our information. The office was a different office.

We hooked up to our spot and attempted to sleep with raindrops playing tympani on the roof. The wind howled. Tito Puente gave us a free concert on the roof. Tito Puente played in Newport, Oregon at the Jazz On The Water Festival, organized by my good friend, Geno, who is a fearsome keyboardist himself. Geno couldn't name his festival "The Newport Jazz Festival" because of copyright infringement of the famous Newport Jazz Festival in Newport, Rhode Island.

Every time I woke that night I heard tapping, a sonic poem like a dark finger from a dripping cedar branch. The rain hung in like a drunken diplomat with a booger. Would we ever find the sun?

The sun was the whole point. Was this a Ray Bradbury story where the sun only shines once every seven years on Venus, or a vacation? The whole philosophy of the Snowbird is to leave the harsh northern climate where you have slaved for years at your Sisyphean job, leave that bone chill, baby, and find a sunny paradise where your troubles evaporate off your lily white skin as you grow your own melanoma farm. I wanted my ultraviolet props.

In the mercy of dawn, I walked outside and saw black clouds. An hour later the clouds cleared, exposing blue sky. I sensed a brighter future.

Barb and I donned swimming suits and walked across a crisp green lawn bordered with palm trees into a sparkling blue pool complex with curved exposed-aggregate patios. We swam laps and enjoyed the relaxing warmth of solar radiation. We soaked in the relaxing electrical radiation of the hot tub. No visitors invaded our private blueness. The oppression of grey skies scurried back into its craven cortical cave. I felt bliss.

We texted pictures to Joshua, back in fungus-heaven Eugene. I wasn't being a Facebook-look-at-me snob since he was coming to Tucson soon. We texted him an interesting sign prohibiting swimmers with diarrhea. Back in the RV, I checked the weather. Another front approached from the West. I had wanted to go up the Palm Springs Aerial Tramway that afternoon, but there were 40 mph winds predicted.

I noticed an ad for Sunnylands, the famous estate of Walter and Leonore Annenberg in Rancho Mirage. I had heard the name many times on NPR radio. The Annenberg Foundation is a major contributor to non-profit educational broadcasting, among other charities, via the Annenberg Corporation for Public Broadcasting. Sunnylands is the Madison-Avenuish name of the lavish Annenberg Estate. I might rename my home Happyville or Smudgepot.

Walter Annenberg made his nut by expanding the family magazine business into radio and television in the 1940s. He created the popular TV Guide and, at one point, owned the Inquirer. He had no fear of brandishing his publishing business to promote his political ideals.

The Annenbergs devoted their wealth to public service and philanthropy. They were tireless hosts. They threw a spectacular New Year's party, attended by the rich and famous. You might run into their good friends the Reagans or the Nixons or the Bushes or the Clintons or the Rat Pack or Bob Hope or any of Hollywood's biggest stars at a Sunnylands event.

The estate takes up an entire square mile and has its own golf course. We visited the elegant Visitor Center outside the main grounds. A running movie informed us of the interesting history of the Annenbergs. Linked garden plots, with meticulously nurtured cacti and succulent species arranged in geometric rows, led around the grounds. The perfect spacing of the rows and the iteration of flawless, healthy succulents made me feel, I don't know, frumpy?

Dark clouds rolled over the San Jacinto Mountains, but we enjoyed a perfect afternoon of desert sunlight. After Sunnylands, we made a Walmart stop and retired to our camp for a nice dinner. The Emerald had great Wi-Fi, a rarity in RV parks, so I hooked up my Amazon Fire and we watched The Good Wife. I made no comments to Barb.

The next morning dawned fair. We made plans to take the Tram in the afternoon. I read books on the sunny lawn of sunny lands and took Waffles out on a leash. She hated the leash. She tangled herself around my chair legs. When I tried to walk her, she planted her paws. The walk turned into a drag. When she tired of being dragged, she collapsed sideways in abject protest. Cats!

Tramway Road leads from the entrance gate at the eastern border of Palm Springs up four steep miles to the base of the Palm Springs Aerial Tramway. Tramway Road is the second steepest bicycle climb in southern California with an average grade of 9.5% and 1.6 miles over 10%. The Pursuit handled the grade well. RV parking was only five slots. We got the last.

The Palm Springs Aerial Tramway, the largest rotating aerial tramway in the world opened in 1963. It ascends North America's steepest canyon, Chino Canyon, 5,873 feet from the Coachella Valley to Mountain Station at the border of Mount San Jacinto State Park. The route traverses five life zones from the Sonoran Desert to alpine forest.

Up canyon, the mountain looms as a solid rock. Chino Canyon is an erosional runway through the Southern California Batholith, a discordant pluton of Mesozoic granite that forms the core of the San Jacinto Mountains. I wonder. I wore shoes called Chinos in high school. They were shit for protecting from Spanish Daggers.

The Cahuilla Indians called Chino Canyon home until they were flooded out in 1860. Settlers named the canyon for Pedro Chino, a Cahuilla shaman who died in 1939 at age one hundred thirteen years. Massive floods are a recurrent theme here. In 1985, a flash flood bulldozed a mile of Tramway Road, burying cars in mud and stranding Tram passengers at Valley Station.

We boarded the 80-person, round aerial tram car in an afternoon chill of fifty degrees. As we rumbled up the mountain, we gazed the alchemy of a rose pink sunset that bathed the entire Coachella Valley. On top, we hiked over hard-frozen, slippery paths to a viewpoint looking over a blanket of lights.

The punctae of dancing lights on a black velvet void made my tripod come erect. I had my carbon fiber Benro tripod and my Nikon D-600 with my favorite lens, a Nikkor 16-35 mm super-wide.

Barb tolerates my photography dance better than do most of my friends. When dramatic scenery surrounds a photographer, walking becomes geriatric. One must stop and pop repeatedly. As one of our guest lecturers at the Portland Photographic Society said, "If you see the shot, you have to stop."

We drove the Pursuit down the ridiculously steep curves

of Tramway Road. I put it in second gear, but had to feather the brakes constantly. When we reached the exit, I smelled pungent brake lining coming through the air vents. The future held much longer challenging descents, but none steeper.

Tomorrow Phoenix. I wanted to see what Quartzite looked like on the way. It had a reputation as a mecca for RVers.

Sunnylands Visitor Center

Coachella Valley from Mountain Station

Christmas in the San Jacintos

Chapter 4

Palm Springs to Phoenix.

Detour to Vietnam

Blue sky morning. I-10 to Phoenix to Bob's house.

Bob, a Marine Corps Vietnam veteran, is a long-time friend who has hosted me and other friends many times at his gracious home in the old horse-lot, flood-irrigated neighborhood of central Phoenix.

It's not a cheap place to live. In 1885, William J. Murphy platted the North Central Corridor with twenty-acre lots: "wherein might be established rural homes at an easy distance from the city." It's hard to imagine this manicured, green inner suburb being any distance from the city that is now a massive, Salt-River-Project-irrigated, sprawling kingdom of the Sonoran Desert grown from the seeds of a Gila-River-irrigated Hohokam town.

Bob's neighborhood still had flood irrigation. Per schedule, you open an underground pipe with a wrench and let water flood your lawn for your permitted time. This will keep your lawn crystal green and your citrus trees fat with hanging, delicious fruit.

Barb and I met and married in Phoenix during our residencies. We lived in a house off 48th and Thomas that had flood irrigation. The bountiful Salt River Project water nurtured grapefruit and Ponderosa limes. We wore rubber boots out in six inches of water to turn off the irrigation, often in the middle of the night. The irritable neighbor downstream always yelled that I was stealing her water.

Another friend, Greg, who grew up with Bob in Phoenix, now lived in Bend, Oregon. I became friends with him, through Bob, and often stayed at his house outside Bend on photography trips to central Oregon. Greg built his house on sixty acres of sage-scented irrigated pasture. A large brick Russian Oven efficiently heated the house. The dining room window framed the snow-covered peaks of the Cascades. Visiting Greg at his bucolic homestead put me in the mind of Tom Bombadil, Tolkien's merry "master of wood, water and hill."

Greg developed a serious cancer and endured major surgery, followed by chemotherapy and radiation. He developed a recurrence, after which he lost confidence in his doctors. Researching the literature, he self-designed his own cancer regimen. He studied the Warburg effect, which states that cancer cells are primarily dependent on glucose for energy, as they lack enzymes to metabolize ketones. He ate a strict zero-glucose, ketogenic diet of kale and green vegetables.

Greg connected with his wife, June, when he emailed lots of old friends during his chemotherapy. June, an elementary-school girlfriend of Greg's from Phoenix, moved to Alaska when she was young. Unbeknown to Greg, June got divorced and had been living in Bend for seven years. When Greg returned to Bend, he moved in with June and they soon married.

The previous summer, Bob and I had visited Greg. At the time of our visit, Greg had lost his body fat, but his untiring brain functioned with vigor. He lived in June's comfortable house in town. We thought he was bed-bound, but, quiet as a cat, he appeared in the living room, looking like Stonehenge in a fog. He launched into a detailed and elegant description of his research, expositing on theories of cancer treatment. It was glorious to watch, like Lincoln giving the Gettysburg Address.

Bob and I camped on Greg's land. Early one morning,

June and Greg drove up. Greg, looking skeletal, walked forthrightly out to his pasture and began disconnecting huge, wheeled irrigation pipes. We scurried to help him. He wanted to winterize his pipes. June told me he insisted on maintaining the pasture throughout his illness. He lacked cows, but he still had his pride. I promised Greg that Bob and I would email him photos of his old family home in Phoenix.

What about Bob? Bob is one of the original Geezers and has been in my inner circle for years. Bob is older than most of us since, while we were high schoolers going on dates to drive-ins, Bob was a Marine Corps battlefield corpsman serving in Vietnam. Bob attended Northern Arizona University, NAU, in Flagstaff, on the GI Bill.

We didn't know what to make of Bob at first. He had PTSD. He dove under his bed in reaction to loud noises. Sometimes his thoughts didn't seem to connect. We Tucson boys bounced back home, to the UofA, after Flagstaff and Bob transferred to Pima Community College. We reconnected. He joined us for hikes and, over time, melded into our circle. Bob drove a full carload of Geezers to the inaugural Yellowstone trip and shot fantastic photos.

For many years Bob never spoke of Vietnam. We were at a high camp in the Whetstone Mountains. Everyone had gone to bed. Bob and I lounged around the campfire and, for the first time, he told me stories of Vietnam. He held forth into the wee hours. Some kind of dam had broken.

Silhouetted by the rose light of dying coals, Bob's raspy bass mingled with the smoke. He told me about Lieutenant John Bobo, who, his leg shattered in a firefight and unable to walk, shoved his bleeding stump into the dirt and covered his platoon as they retreated. Later, I read the citation on the Congressional Medal of Honor website. That was one of the stories.

On I-10 we drove through Quartzite. It looked spectacularly uninviting from the freeway. We kept going.

Barb had remained active in Joshua's Boy Scout troop after he earned his Eagle. As secretary, she performed many duties. She dropped and shattered her iPhone while texting with troop friends upset about the latest scouting snafu. She was frantic. I said, "Why don't you tell them you are on vacation and get someone else to deal with it." Barb replied, with mock seriousness, "No, I am indispensable!"

We couldn't park the Photon Bus, my christened name for the Pursuit, in Bob's driveway because of an old oak tree that guarded the entrance. The Bus is twelve feet high to the top of the air conditioners. We parked in the street.

Bob flees the intense Phoenix heat every summer and drives around America in his Lexus hybrid, visiting reunions of fellow marines and touring interesting places. One summer he returned home and discovered six inches of standing water flooding the house from a broken pipe.

He remodeled his genteel home with a modern, bright decor, which may explain why Bob freaked out when the cat came in. Waffles, catlike, explored Bob's house. Bob followed her. At every room, I heard Bob say, "Don't go in there. Don't go in there." I realized Bob just wasn't a cat person. Sorry Waffles, but it's back to the Bus.

After sipping fine aged cognac we headed out to a nice Mexican restaurant. Barb told Bob about her iPhone dilemma. After dinner, Bob drove us to a Verizon store, open late for Christmas. Barb got a new iPhone 7. I said, "Merry Christmas."

We took our tripods over to Greg's parent's old house and shot long exposures of the neighborhood, aglow with Christmas lights. June emailed that Greg got a big lift seeing his old childhood neighborhood.

A brand new Sony 4K flat screen sat, like a grinning Buddha, on Bob's new hardwood floor. After a while, I pointed out that there was no credenza! Bob said he admired my glass credenza at home. The next morning we trooped over to Best Buy and bought a mahogany-and-glass credenza that accented nicely with Bob's decor. New phone. New credenza. We are forever reversing entropy.

After our relaxing visit with Bob, we headed south on I-10 into the maelstrom of a family Christmas. Forget Christmas, the Gnomanium was coming, the big party we would have at Steve's house. Steve and I had been friends ever since our freshman year at NAU.

We organized the gathering over many emails. I sent out eighty invitations, which made him nervous. He suggested it should be my retirement party. I constructed the name Gnomanium, which referred to my old nickname, the Gnome, and also to the Seinfeld episode where Neuman called his New Year's party the Neumanium. No one got it. I repeatedly explained the origin of the name. Exasperating plebeians. Some jokes beg for interment.

Bob in Vietnam

Greg and June on Paulina Peak

CHAPTER 5

HOMEWARD BOUND

When I was 16 years old, my family moved from Fort Worth, Texas to Tucson, where my father, Bill Sr., took the reins as manager of the Merrill Lynch office. My youngest brother, Jim, is about to finish his career at the same office and his son, Jimmy, now works there along with his best friend, Alex. I watched Jimmy and Alex grow up. There is comfort having family members watch over your money.

I was heading home. Although I've lived in Portland for 30 years, I still consider Tucson my home. As the saying goes, it's where my heart is.

In Texas, were part of a large extended family. In Arizona, it was just the six of us. I remember both apprehension and excitement moving away from the only home I had known to an exotically different location.

The Sonoran Desert is a stark contrast to the oak-covered hills and green farmlands of Texas. But, as Arizonans will tell you, the desert will grow on you. With time, your senses imprint with magnificent orange sunsets and the euphoric ozone smell of the desert after a monsoon rain. Now, after years of exploring the desert places, the caves and the canyons, the sky-island mountains, the grasslands and cienegas, Arizona is in my blood. If you took Arizona away from me, I wouldn't have any blood.

My mother, Anne, lives in the house we moved into forty-six years ago in the Harold Bell Wright Estates. Harold Bell Wright (1872-1944), a Methodist pastor, wrote several major novels. The Shepherd of the Hills is his best-known work and a movie starring John Wayne. Set in Branson, Missouri, the novel transformed Branson into a tourist destination.

Wright lived at his Tucson estate from 1914 to 1933. The street names in the neighborhood derive from his fictional characters. My mother's home is on Shepherd Hills Drive and connects with Brian Kent and Printer Udell. These characters now get along and connect well.

We picked up a rental car in north Tucson at the smallest agency I've ever seen. It had the best price.

At Mom's, I prepared myself for a potential tussle as to where we would park the Photon Bus. My parents had parked their Bounder outside the garage by a landscaped island. I presumed I would park there.

No! My mother wanted me to park in a narrow side driveway that led to my father's wood shop. I worried it would be too narrow. It wasn't, but I had to hunt for a spot that didn't open into the loving arms of a jumping cholla or prickly pear. I found a water hydrant, so we had water. A long extension cord from the shop supplied power. Full hook up!

My parents bought the Bounder after my father started his second career doing consulting work for NASDAQ, which required travel to businesses around the country. After the consulting job, they downsized to a twenty-two-foot Lazy Days Class C. After my first trip in a big Class A, I understand their desire to downsize.

At thirty-one feet, the Pursuit is a small Class A, yet it looks enormous compared to our old Catalina. Parking requires two usual-sized automobile spaces end-to-end, whereas sometimes I could park the Catalina at an angle into a single space.

We encountered nightmare driving scenarios. Once, when pulling out into traffic, Barb cried out in alarm, making me think someone was coming. I stopped immediately. The car behind me pulled to my rear. I was stuck. The Bus blocked a lane and a half in the path of oncoming traffic. The traffic veered around me, every driver honking in anger. The driver behind me never backed up. I wondered which car would slam into our mid section.

Another time we pulled into a Whole Foods lot only to find the entire lot full, with narrow lanes and many pedestrians. We inched our way to the back of the lot, scanning for a spot large enough for a three-point turn. The lot mercifully connected to an alley with just enough clearance.

As the trip progressed, I scanned any parking lot we entered, looking for routes through, exits and parking spaces large enough for our rig. We encountered roads with vehicle length limited to, say, twenty feet or twenty-eight feet. Several roads in Death Valley have vehicle limits, including the beautiful Artist's Drive.

How many RV owners end up downsizing? I failed to find an exact number, but smaller RVs are selling better. An article on letsrv.com stated the Class B market shot up by 18.9% in the first four months of 2015, with smaller increases for Class A, 7.8%, and Class C, 14.9%. This may not be due to downsizers, as Millennials, a rising RV-purchasing population, have a greater taste for the sportier, more maneuverable Class B.

For better or worse, we had upsized. As the family arrived, I proudly gave tours of the Bus. They would say the supportive thing, "Oooooh, this is NICE!", followed by, "How do you drive this thing?"

Years ago, my parents visited us in their Bounder. They and my Uncle Bud and Aunt MaryJo and other friends caravanned to our house in Clackamas. Uncle Bud, who spent his career building Boeing 747 tail sections, converted a Dodge van into a Class B with all the works. We parked all three RVs in our driveway. We toured the wine country, barbecued on the porch and played golf.

At the time of that trip, Dad's Alzheimer's was progressing

despite experimental drug trials at the University of Arizona. He left his hat at the golf course. We drove back to get it. My father, a very hard-working, intelligent, humorous and caring man, kept apologizing for forgetting his hat and making me drive back to the course. It broke my heart. His admiring colleagues spoke the words, "a fair man," repeatedly at his retirement party.

Even with a fading memory, he still drove the big Bounder. However, on the trip back to Tucson, Mom had to take the wheel. He became confused about exit ramps and which strip of concrete was actually the road. The next couple of years, as Dad's mind devolved and left only an emaciated body with no light in the eyes, were the hardest and saddest chapter of our family history. I visited as often as I could in the torrent of a busy schedule in those days.

I have no desire to watch *Still Alice* or any of the other heartbreaking movies about Alzheimer's, except for *I'll Be Me*, which was more about the exceptional Glen Campbell than about heartbreak. During Dad's decline, I experienced nothing good or uplifting.

One incident, though, gave me a small slice of happiness. After retirement, Dad built a well-appointed wood shop where he spent hours creating attractive sculptures that my mother would paint. These sculptures still bless our home. After a certain point, Mom deemed him no longer safe to work in the wood shop. On one of my visits I took him out to the shop. We made a propeller-on-a-stick toy. When we flew it, Dad giggled with delight every time it took off. I realized, with pain and joy, that I was seeing my father, the man who had raised me through the good and bad, as a five-year-old.

Mom arranged the families in her house like old puzzle pieces. My sister's family came in from Texas and Los Angeles. Waffles was 86ed from the house because, Maggie, my sister's sweet natured Golden Retriever, was there. Waffles seemed perfectly content in the Bus with its many large windows.

A perfect storm of events: runway construction, bad weather and a bomb scare, stranded Joshua and his girlfriend at LAX. We collected them in Phoenix the next day. Brother John's family couldn't make it from California. We celebrated Christmas with all the usual: jubilant voices, great cooking, games, puzzles, pool table challenges, white elephant presents, hikes and golf.

Golf. My brother-in-law, Richard, who builds luxury homes in Dallas, is a single-digit handicap. He always beats us. Just months before, Richard suffered a central retinal artery occlusion and lost most of the vision in one eye. He had difficulty with depth perception. I beat him for the first time out at 49er's Country Club, but I took no pride. Richard, gentleman that he is, commented that my game had improved. It had, but I'm pretty sure when he learns how to compensate, it will be my last victory.

Christmas flowed and ebbed on a tide of voices. The decibel level in Mom's house dropped with every goodbye. The Gnomanium loomed. After consulting with Steve, I ran around town buying supplies for the party.

In our college days at NAU Steve had a bombproof, faded old Toyota Landcruiser. We cruised back roads around Flagstaff through Ponderosa Pines.

Steve likes to tell the story of the Jack-In-The-Box incident. We passengers were overly cheerful on beer when Steve pulled into the Jack. He tried to order, but we kept screaming epithets at the menu speaker, laughing hysterically. "Hey Jack, fuck you." Yes, Steve, we were all young once.

Steve, a successful business management expert, used to travel constantly working for Raytheon, IBM, Six Sigma and others. He and his wife, Monica, a former executive at the University of Phoenix, are in the throes of raising three teenage daughters. They are surviving.

Steve is a master gardener. Around his pool he has color gardens with lots of annuals, but outside the walls he constructed a flagstone fire pit in the desert xeriscape. At Christmas, the lights of the Tucson Valley blend into the seasonal lights of the neighborhood. To sum it up, Steve's house is a great place for a party. We Geezers often call Steve when we get in town and suggest getting together, knowing that our openhearted friend will say, "Why don't you all come over to my house. I'll cook carne seca." We can't say no, can we?

I started the process early this trip, speaking at length with Steve about the details of the party. He suggested this be my retirement party. I came up with the name, Gnomanium. Steve was nervous about how many would attend. I invited eighty, but many were out of town. I attempted to alleviate Steve's anxiety by saying, "I don't know, anywhere from twenty to sixty." Steve brought up the Jack-In-The-Box incident.

Before the trip, I practiced my guitar and harmonica. I'm not a pro musician. My vocals are, perhaps, serviceable. I have not spent the ten thousand hours one needs to become a master musician. I spent far more hours training to become a competent surgeon. Physician, not musician.

I love playing. During my mid-career burnout, I pursued the joyful stress reduction of songwriting. The Portland Songwriter's Association, where I did time as vice president, sponsored monthly showcases at venues around Portland. Professional musicians judged us wannabes at the performances. It was a worth a bruised ego to play for a crowd.

If we had flown out, I would not have been able to bring my favorite Martin DX1 Dreadnaught guitar, harmonica case, Fishman Loudbox Mini Acoustic amplifier, Zoom A3 Acoustic Guitar Preamp and Effects Processor, Shure SM58 mic, mic stand, pop screen and collapsible music stand. One more advantage of RV travel over flying.

I worked out charts for over a hundred songs, favorites from the 70s and 80s like Tom Petty, Neil Young, Cat Stevens and early Bob Dylan songs, inspired by Bob's Nobel Prize. My performance bones were brittle. The chance to play a gig enlivened me even if it was a party with friends. Hey, as the song goes, you git it while you can.

To quote a beloved character, the Gnomanium was the best time of my life. It was a joyful evening punctuated by high-spirited voices. The rain stopped. The stars, above and below, joined the party. About thirty people showed, so Steve relaxed and enjoyed the ignition of old friends. Bob drove down from Phoenix.

I set up a stage in front of Steve's hot tub. His pet desert tortoises lived behind the hot tub. They were still hibernating and didn't seem to mind. The six baby tortoises lived above the garage, among an epiphytic splendor of orchids.

The Gnomanium was a night of friends and joy. Howard, an excellent player, joined in with his Martin. Lew, an old friend from high school and another Tucson returnee, who I hadn't seen in years, popped in with his engaging wife. Everyone joined in for vocals on American Pie.

Mom told me the next day, "I didn't expect to have a good time, but I did." Yes, it was the best time of my life, among other best times.

Then it was over. We stayed a few more days at Mom's house. She mentioned, several times, "There's a nice park on Pantano." We got the clue. One nice thing about RVs, you can leave any time.

I inspected the park on Pantano. It was a sunken, viewless concrete lot. The RVs, stained and peeling, nearly touched each other. Large white letters labeled each site like some kind of work camp. I expected to see Henry Fonda drive up in a Model T full of Okies. Was my mother punishing me?

A Google search popped up a map of Tucson with many more RV park options. I wanted to visit the Arizona Sonora Desert Museum. A campground close to the Museum had only dry camping. I saw a nearby park, The Desert Trails RV Park. The website stated, "We attract an energetic customer base." Energetic customers sounded uplifting, and the price was reasonable. When Mom and Barb returned from church, I had the Bus packed and ready to go.

Steve's patio and fire pit in the Tucson Foothills

Howard jams with me at the Gnomanium

Invitation to the Gnomanium. We were younger once.
Steve in center, seated.

CHAPTER 6

TIN CUP AND THE SONORAN DESERT

The Desert Trails RV Park was off Ajo Highway ten miles west of I-19. I was far less familiar with the west side of Tucson, so I felt a mild sense of exploration seeing new areas. The Park had a friendly feel to it. I scanned the area looking for the energetic customer base. We backed into a graveled site with a picnic table, with plenty of room to park the rental car. Christmas lawn figures and string lights adorned many sites of seasonal roosters.

We hooked up, leveled, and explored the camp, finding a good-sized lending library where we picked out a DVD of Longmire and a season of NCIS. We made dinner, watched some Longmire, and turned in early. The sky was grey, but not raining.

The next morning I realized I wouldn't be taking Waffles out on her leash. Out the windshield, a parade of dog-walkers flowed by in a continuous loop, like Westminster for mixed breeds. I wondered if every camper had a dog with them. On the walk to the showers everyone I passed smiled and said, "Good Morning." This was a friendly camp. I wondered if there would be some kind of initiation ceremony.

We golfed at the Tubac Golf Resort and Spa. Tubac is forty miles south of Tucson, just north of Tumacacori. You know the place. This is the course where they filmed the U.S. Open Qualifying rounds for the movie Tin Cup with Kevin Costner. I heard from friends that Costner cut a wide swath through Tucson. Every night.

We Tucson boys used to go down to Tubac in the summer to play golf in pre-Tin Cup days. Tubac was even hotter and more humid than Tucson, which kept the course clear of normal people. We liked the price: eighteen dollars for eighteen holes with a cart, and they threw in a steak dinner. Since we had the course to ourselves, we could jump into the water holes to cool off.

Barb is learning to play golf. I never could get her to come out with me, but last summer her Bible study group played every Tuesday and her friends gave her lessons. Thank God for that.

The streets surrounding the pleasant rouge-bricked territorial style clubhouse were named from the Tin Cup movie. The place had been Tin-Cupified. A sales-pitch friendly pro shop man and smiling starters got us quickly into the course. They gave us ice water in styrofoam cups. I wondered why we were the only group playing that day on a twenty-seven hole course. Where were the other snowbirds on this perfect day in high season? Curious.

They say that southern Arizona and the border towns have changed over time with the rise of the cartels. In high school, we would tootle down I-19 and cross the border for exotic Hemingway-themed dinners at La Caverna or other affordable restaurants in Nogales, which was always well-lit and festive with lots of tourists. Now, they tell me, no one goes to Nogales any more except for dental work, which has become one of the few successful businesses in the border towns.

I don't know, but I can't shake the sensation that everything always changes for the worse. Maybe it's a biologic phenomenon. We have more dopamine in our brains when we're young. Does that explain why memories from youth are brighter and rose-hued? I don't know. I'm not a Neurologist.

After a pleasant round in perfect weather on the well-manicured course, we drove into the galleried tourist mall streets of Tubac to look for a good restaurant. Only one restaurant was open. Dozens of shops and galleries had already closed. It was early evening. Curiouser and curiouser! The Mexican food was delicious, but over-priced, fifty dollars for two. I griped about this to anyone who would listen during the rest of the trip until Barb got sick of hearing it.

The next morning was bright blue sky. There's magic in early desert mornings. We beelined it to the Arizona Sonora Desert Museum. The Museum is spectacular. It's one of those places you take every out-of-town visitor.

I majored in Biology at the University of Arizona. In high school, I did a year-long field project and gave presentations at elementary schools with my friend Joe Kittinger, who's father formerly held the world record for the highest skydive.

In the course of those studies I learned how to run plant transects and rodent traplines. I caught many snakes, rattlers and bull snakes, driving the back roads at night. I caught them live with a snake stick, except the time my friend, Raul Bazurto, drove my old Corvair sixty on a dirt road and couldn't stop in time. Mom tired of finding snakes in her freezer. One time, at the base of Mount Lemmon, during a plant survey, I heard a loud rattle, seeming to originate from everywhere. I located the massive Diamondback's head perched on the top of a prickly pear three feet off the ground.

In the ague of Oregon winter my mind often wanders the aisles of my Arizona memories. Last winter I bought a used copy of *A Natural History of the Sonoran Desert*, published by the Museum Press, to have as a reference. This thick tome is a detailed, comprehensive guide to all aspects of the Sonoran natural world, authored by a rich list of distinguished naturalists. I perused it and, before I knew it, I had read it from cover to cover. It unearthed a lot of buried knowledge from my biology days. I kindled a daydream of becoming a docent at the Museum.

The Arizona-Sonora Desert Museum, founded in 1952, is a ninety-eight acre zoo, aquarium, botanical garden, natural history museum, publisher and art gallery. It is fourteen miles west of downtown Tucson. The unique quality of the Museum is that the grounds blend into the 24,818 acres of the Saguaro National Monument, Tucson Mountain District. Few zoos blend into pristine nature, where you can walk right out and see the free, wild cousins of the zoo-bound species. You can't walk out of the San Diego Zoo into the African Savannah.

The smiling woman at the ticket booth told us we had enough time to make the raptor flights on Desert Loop Trail. She seemed excited. I've seen raptor flights where the raptor flies from one gauntleted handler to another. Surprisingly, it was OK for me to take my tripod. It is getting difficult to find any public venue where photographers may bring tripods.

We made our way through the aquarium, reptiles, invertebrates, and amphibians, over the scenic overlook and into the Earth Sciences Center cave. The Museum is famous for realistic concrete reproductions of natural rock and caves. I shot from the tripod as we walked. The brilliant, fluorescent, multicolored specimens in the mineral gallery looked great in long exposures. We perambled by the mountain lion, the Mexican wolves and Cat Canyon and made it in time to see the raptor free flight. I'm glad we did.

They should advertise: Not your grandmother's raptor flight. The raptor handlers brought out, in succession, a Peregrine Falcon, a Barn Owl and a family of Harris Hawks. Upon release, these hunters of the sky flew random patterns around a several-hundred-yard area. They flew right at us at eye level, pulling up just in time. Several times Harris Hawk wings brushed my forehead. Exhilarating.

Our group got an unexpected bonus. A wild Harris Hawk flew into the area and started hunting. The zoo's hawks joined in and, like a shot, the entire family pounced on a rodent and tore it to bits. The handler told us that was not part of the program. Sorry, rodent.

I put my Nikon on continuous shooting mode and pre-focused on what I thought would be a good distance for most shots. That was a mistake. I should have kept the auto-focus on, but I didn't realize the raptors would fly inches from my lens. I managed to click a few keepers.

Docents stalked every sidewalk, like out-of-work department store Santas. Some spieled out professorial trail-side tutorials, but most walked around, Secret Service style, with their lanyards displayed. I got the impression they spent most of their day telling kids not to throw pebbles at the animals. My miniature dream of becoming a docent cracked and spilled itself on the desert caliche.

Zoo blends into the Desert

Handler with Harris Hawk

Harris Hawks hunting

Peregrine Falcon

Chapter 7

Santa Fe - Half The Way

My friend, Rick, lives in Santa Fe. Rick and I were apartment mates at the University of Arizona and became best of friends. We had many adventures back then with our fellow outdoor enthusiasts, who have evolved into the so-called Geezers.

Both of us left Tucson to seek our fortunes. I left for medical school. Rick wandered into a small town in Texas on the Brazos River, Fort Bend, where he became editor of the local newspaper. He lived in a cow pasture in a trailer. Jay and I visited him in that pasture. Elvis Presley died that day. It was also my birthday.

He lived in San Diego for a while where he learned to be a mechanic, returned to Tucson, built his own house, and got married. His wife found it difficult to connect with Tucson and she loved Boston, so they moved to Providence, Rhode Island, where Rick worked for many years at the Brown University Book Store, in charge of computer sales. He loved that job. He brushed elbows with Nobel Prize winners and celebrities, like Dustin Hoffman, whose kids attended Brown.

Rick's wife moved to Santa Fe to care for her aging mother, so Rick packed up and moved yet again. His wife's mother developed multiple suspicious ailments whenever Rick's wife was around and it drove the wife nuts, so she moved to Connecticut. Rick stayed in the intoxicating climate of Santa Fe where he is now a Level III Systems Analyst at Santa Fe Community College.

Barb and I frequently call Rick to help with our computer problems. He has spent hours fixing our computers. I asked him if we could visit him in Santa Fe and park the Bus in the abandoned tennis court next to his house. He said sure, but he warned us about his narrow driveway.

We left Tucson on a perfect day, seventies, bright blue sky. We drove to the small rental office to turn in our car. No one was there. We waited. I walked into the back office. A young girl was on a tattered couch watching TV. It looked like a small army had trashed the place. The girl said her dad was out. On my second foray she mentioned the drop box out front.

We headed east on I-10, a route I had driven many times. When I was in high school, I had a job at a factory near the airport that made metal doors and windows. It was a troglodyte job, no offense to troglodytes. I had to drive past an entrance ramp to I-10. I would look up at that green freeway sign and think, one day I will drive up that ramp and just keep going, which is what I did when I drove I-10 to medical school in Atlanta. After I left for medical school, I never lived in Tucson. Here I was again leaving my hometown on a perfectly beautiful day.

We stopped at the Texas Canyon rest stop east of Tucson. In the 1880's, Texas immigrants camped at the pass and people said, "There's a bunch of damned Texans up there." The scenic boulders have vied for Grammys in Hollywood cowboy movies.

Texas Canyon is a pass between the Little Dragoon Mountains and the Dragoon Mountains. We friends camped in Cochise Stronghold in the Dragoons where people say Cochise is buried.

Approaching the Canyon, out your windshield, you see a giant's playground of boulders, pink granite porphyry and tan quartz monzonite porphyry, with large crystals of feldspar and banded gneiss, all showing spheroidal weathering and exfoliation, or, in the common vernacular, big rocks.

I'm a geology enthusiast, but I can't claim deep knowledge. I've re-read most of John McPhee's excellent geology writings, including Annals of the Former World, which happened to be in the bookshelf. McPhee takes obvious delight in disgorging exotic and arcane geology language, but his writing is so brilliantly fluent that one is willing to surf that subduction.

In New Mexico we resupplied at a Walmart in Deming. RV travelers learn that parking is never a problem at a Walmart, which has catered to the RV world by allowing overnight camping in some stores. The Palm Springs Walmart does not allow camping. They communicated that unequivocally by swarming the Bus with security cars. Each Walmart store manager decides whether to allow camping. You can Google Walmart Locator and find out which stores allow camping.

From Deming we took the shortcut up NM 26, freshly paved, to the town of Hatch, famous for delicious, popular chilies and the Hatch New Mexico Chili Festival. On the roadside, we saw a police car, adorned with flowers and American flags. I later learned the story of Officer Jose Chavez. Chavez, a naturalized U.S. citizen and highly respected law enforcement officer, pulled over a Lexus for a traffic violation. One of the drug runners in the Lexus shot him. The decorated police cruiser was a monument to Chavez.

It got dark around Elephant Butte on I-25 and once again I had to deal with the pathetic low beams whenever there was oncoming traffic. We found a park in Socorro on Google and booked it. The woman, similar to the one at the Emerald in Palm Springs, gave me detailed instructions on what to do if no one was at the camp office.

It turned out the office was a beauty shop doing double duty. We left our fee in the drop box and found a spot on the dusty, gravel lot. There were full hook ups. The next morning I saw a row of ancient, deteriorating motorhomes. It was a funky camp, but the night's sleep was equitably pleasant.

The next day we drove under dark, threatening skies to Santa Fe. I found a glass repair outfit to fix a chip in the windshield. The new insurance covered it although it took multiple calls to find the right insurance person. Incompetent bureaucracy is the bane of American life.

We pulled up to Rick's driveway. There were trees on both sides of the anemic lane and a low brick wall. It looked impossible. I hacked tree branches with my knife, which sprained my wrist. With Barb giving signals from the front, I inched trough the labyrinth, scratching the side on some branches. Rick advised me to put the Bus next to his front deck instead of the tennis court. I backed into a snug fit under an old juniper.

The trip from Tucson had been tiring. My neck was sore. I could relax now, knowing we had several days to explore Santa Fe without having to drive the big rig. Who knew how long we would stay.

It snowed that night. After dinner, we watched a Longmire episode in the Bus. Unlike my mother and Bob, Rick allowed Waffles into his home, although he was nervous about having the whammy box in his dining nook. As a selling point, I told him he wouldn't have to worry about mice for a while.

Rick is fastidious, neat and organized. He keeps track of every milligram of sodium in his diet for fear of developing high blood pressure, which he doesn't have. Barb checked his BP with a cuff. He was fine.

He offered to let me drive his old Nissan. I started it and let it warm up as instructed. Dude, there's no clutch! Even with the clutch pedal pressed to the floor, the gears crunched and the car took off. It stalled whenever I hit the brake. Where is the damn clutch?

I gave up and declared I would rent a car. Even if I could have overcome the learning curve, I didn't want to risk a breakdown somewhere in northern New Mexico. Rick feigned exasperation I was unable to drive the Nissan. "It's easy. You just have to let it warm up." As long-time friends, we entertain ourselves with mutual harassment.

The snow came down crisp and dry as it does in the Rockies. The Photon Bus was as welcoming as a meat locker. Rick let us take over his big bedroom. We slept in sleeping bags with Waffles sandwiched in between.

We developed a daily routine with Rick. Barb and I would go touring somewhere during the day and then pick up dinner items at one of three designated grocery stores. We would make dinner and then watch one Seinfeld episode on Hulu on Rick's computer. He didn't want to watch more than one so he could spread out the series. I understood that.

The first day was a Saturday so Rick didn't have to work. We drove to Taos in the rental car. The streets of Santa Fe had hard-frozen snow, but NM 68 was clear.

In Taos, the San Francisco de Asis Mission Church is a magnet for tourists. This thick adobe structure, built by Franciscans, no doubt with the help of the local labor, in 1815, is one of many churches built by Spaniard colonizers in New Mexico. The Mission is a compelling image, painted by Georgia O'Keeffe and photographed by Ansel Adams. I add my name to the list.

I have two framed Ansel Adams prints in my home. One is Moonrise, Hernandez, New Mexico, his most popular and iconic image. In this ethereal image the moon rises over a cemetery of glowing white crosses outside an adobe church. A layer of low cirrocumulus clouds on the horizon glows white as if supernaturally illuminated. The top half of the print is a starless black void. Moonrise is a photographic essay about mortality and timelessness. I thought about visiting the site at Hernandez, which is a few miles from Espanola. However, according to several online posts, mature trees now hide the cemetery and church. In a few days I would find my own Moonrise-style photo.

After exploring the Mission, we ate at Rick's favorite Mexican restaurant and then headed out to the Rio Grande Gorge. Over time, Rick had taken a number of visitors on his Taos tour. The high bridge over the Gorge, frozen stiff in a howling, biting wind, offered a seductive panorama, so I shuffled over the ice to get my shots. Done.

A few miles down the road we entered the land of the strange and forlornly beautiful Earthships. The valley welcomes you like the Kingdom of Rohan from The Lord of the Rings. The first Earthship, built in 1979, named The Hobbit House, debuted as an off the grid, self-powered, waste-neutral home.

Architect Michael Reynolds birthed his concept of grid independence in this lonely valley in the 1970s and called it, The Greater World Earthship Community, no doubt causing orgasms in Scientologists. The Ships sail without external energy or well water, generating energy from solar and wind sources and moderating temperature by passive convection. Rainwater is stored and filtered. Plants bio-filter grey water, used for flushing toilets. The black water becomes garden compost. Locally available materials, typically rammed-earth-tires and discarded bottles and cans, artfully integrate the exteriors. South-facing windows transmit heat to passive indoor greenhouses.

I felt a stark, musical beauty gazing over the mountain-rimmed, snow-filled valley home of the Earthships. I was gleefully spastic shooting the exotic imagery.

Rick commented, "There's no trees here." I think we all had the same inner thought: Could I live here? Rick's comment saved us from anxiety. We all agreed we couldn't live without at least some trees. I would not have to agonize over the thought that I should sell everything in Oregon and move to an Earthship in New Mexico.

San Francisco de Asis Mission Church

Earthship outside of Taos

Bridge over the Rio Grande Gorge

Passive Solar Greenhouse

Chapter 8

Georgia O'Keeffe's Art Is Not Vaginal

    Sunday Rick had errands to do, so Barb and I explored Santa Fe. Barb thought maybe she had been to Santa Fe with her family as a kid. She wasn't sure. "I can't remember things," she said with a sigh.
    We entered the plaza through one of the surrounding shopping moats. Stop! Belts! I'm a sucker for southwestern style belts. Sure enough, I bought one. We made it to the street without brandishing another credit card and took in the Cathedral Basilica of Saint Francis of Assisi.
    I sensed a target rich environment. My big black Nikon sat in the car, whining like a scolded child. After lugging the Nikon ten miles in Montana, I purchased a cigarette-box-size Sony RX100 II. The Sony, with its 20.2 megapixels and 1-inch sensor makes acceptable images, but they can't match the resolution from my 24.3 megapixel Nikon D-600. The Nikon has a full frame sensor and the large DSLR lenses allow more light to enter. Hence, the Nikon harvests more photons. Like a backdoor Buddhist, I'm willing to compromise resolution for comfort.
    The Sony is so small and light I hardly notice it. Careful Lebowski, there's a camera here. I made a strap out of climber's webbing. The webbing loops around my neck such that the camera sits at belt-level on my left side. I can quickly bring the camera to eye level. I sported a cross-draw holster in my Single Action Shooter Society days and the motion to draw up the Sony is the same. My alias in SASS was Sody Pop Kid. I stole that name

from Dustin Hoffman's character in Little Big Man.

You don't see art in Santa Fe, you drink it. Art permeates the DNA of every stuccoed facade. Purchasable art thumped our skulls from myriad glass-shiny gallery stores, quaint assemblies of silver and fur and ceramic not for the faint of wallet. I felt faintly queasy wondering if I should offer to buy Barb an overpriced treasure of memory.

I kept my chivalry in check until we entered the long portico along the Palace of Governors where licensed Native American vendors sold their art. The Natives sat behind their creations, displayed on colorful blankets along the redbrick paseo. We strolled the bejeweled aisle. Most of the vendors barely looked up. It was pleasantly low pressure. It was enticingly low-priced. "Barb, why don't you get something?"

Barb crouched down to examine turquoise earrings. I squinted at the price tag. Fourteen dollars! Here was my chance. "Go ahead. Get those." We bought items from several congenial sellers for about a tenth of what one gallery item would have cost. The Natives chatted with us like slow talking neighbors, so different from the whip-smart, prancing sales carnivores in the galleries. My cheapero soul crawled back into its modestly decorated cave.

After the Plaza, we meandered through unpretentious neighborhoods to the Georgia O'Keeffe Museum. Like most people who have a shallow understanding of art, my mental reflex to O'Keeffe was a pavloved image of a flower that looked like a vagina. We males have a certain brain chemistry. Thanks to the Museum, I may emerge from my bleak chrysalis as a more enlightened, aware being, at least regarding my understanding of O'Keeffe.

We almost missed the entrance of the modest adobe house-size Museum. There was an informational film, A Life In Art, narrated by Gene Hackman. (Hackman impressed Barb.) We wandered through a labyrinth of exhibition rooms organized by phases of her career, from her early works at the Art Institute of Chicago to her transformational years at the University of Virginia, where she absorbed Arthur Wesley Dow's philosophy of abstractionism.

Georgia O'Keeffe went through many styles of art in her life cycle. She drew exacting architectural renderings in her younger days. She pleasingly abstracted monolithic New York skyscrapers in the ego-shrinking City Night. By the time she migrated to and bonded with New Mexico, she was years into her inner exploration of emotion-based interpretation of the visual world.

Yes, many of her flowers look like vaginas. Many don't. Here's what she had to say about that: "When people read erotic symbols into my painting, they're really thinking about their own affairs." Well, that and a certain induced physiologic reaction. She birthed her unique vision from her flowered depths in a diversity of subjects, far more than magnolias and cow skulls. My eyes saw and my senses inhaled this poignant story of art as the womb of a life.

One of O'Keeffe's rare sculptures, Abstraction, sat apart on a pedestal like a lost child. A sign stated visitors were inspired to post photographs of the sculpture, inspired by the light and shadows cast on the window shade. The sign asked visitors to share their images on Instagram. Inspiration enveloped me like a rare mist. I made images and designed an abstracted version of Abstraction. I tried to post on Instagram, but without a Millennial to hold my hand it was hopeless.

At the Governors Palace, Santa Fe Plaza

How do I post this on Instagram?

Art is everywhere in Santa Fe

Chapter 9

Los Alamos: beautiful town, ugly bomb.

I got up at 4:00 am this morning to get ready for my flight to Phoenix. As I was brushing my teeth Barb walked in and asked me what I was doing. "We've got to leave by 4:30," I said. "No we don't," she replied, "Your flight is not until 6:00 pm THIS EVENING." I rushed downstairs and looked at my ticket. Sure enough, I had bought pm instead of am. I was mortified.

After our Santa Fe excursion we went back to Rick's, where Barb cooked a delicious chili recipe she had seen in the Santa Fe New Mexican. After dinner we watched an episode of Seinfeld, then Rick clicked on his favorite animated series, a sitcom where many of the characters have animal heads. The main character, who has a horse's head, was a burnt out actor who had a hit series years ago. Barb turned in early.

The next morning, after a relaxing breakfast, Barb and I took off for Los Alamos. I had wanted to visit Los Alamos ever since I read *The Making of the Atomic Bomb*. Richard Rhodes' detailed and well-researched history explores the evolution of nuclear physics and examines the serendipitous nexus of deep thinkers who created the first atomic bomb. This is historical writing at its finest.

We headed north up US Route 84 and took the exit for

NM 502. Something caught my eye. It was the Jemez Mountains, glowing in the distance under a brooding cape of dark, wooly clouds. The vista reminded me of something. We pulled over at a good vantage point. The sunrise was behind my back. I framed the mountains in my viewfinder.

Like many landscape photography enthusiasts, I am an admirer of the great Ansel Adams. He captured his most famous image, Moonrise, Hernandez, New Mexico, about thirty miles from where we were standing.

On October 31, 1941, Adams was driving through the Chama River Valley on a photographic road trip around the western states. Just before 4:00 pm he noticed something, a church and a cemetery. What stopped him was "a twilight glow on the distant peaks and clouds" above the Sangre de Cristo Mountains.

He pulled over and, in great haste, could expose only one image in the dying light. He couldn't find his Weston exposure meter, so he estimated the exposure using the known luminance of the moon, 250 foot-candles. He corrected for the Wratten No. 15 (G) filter and exposed his ASA 64 film in his 8x10 camera for 1 second at f/32. The small aperture ensured a wide depth of field so everything would be in focus.

Last week I was in Tucson and I visited the Center for Creative Photography at the University of Arizona. Parking had been a real problem when I was a student, forty-five years ago. Now, there was a large parking structure across Speedway.

Founded in 1975, the Center germinated from the vision of then-president John P. Schaefer, an accomplished photographer in his own right, and Ansel Adams, who wanted a repository for his works. The Center archives all negatives created by Ansel Adams and curates over two thousand prints and other documents. This is the place to go if you want to research Adams.

I assumed I would find a gallery rich with Ansel Adams prints. Wrong. The young woman at the desk explained that all of

Adams' materials were in the archives. Only graduate students or those with special permission could go there. There was, she said, a current exhibit that had one Adam's photo in it. She added that there were a few drawers in a side room with some archival materials.

I perused the exhibition rooms and found Adams' photograph, the nightstand of a Japanese-American WWII GI, who was the son of a family sent to an internment camp. I found the archival drawers and looked at original prints of John Schaefer's remarkable photos of Mission San Xavier del Bac. I saw a drawer below labeled as "Ansel Adams." There were a few portraits.

I headed to the exit and chatted with the young woman, telling her I was disappointed I didn't get to see more of Adams' original materials. She mentioned there were some additional trays below the one I had seen, including one that had his Moonrise picture. I mentally jolted and followed her back. I had not seen the lower drawers. I opened the tray and found I was staring at the original negative and original contact print of Moonrise, Hernandez, New Mexico.

The contact print was nothing like the image in my hallway. In this original print the sky is overexposed and clouds are visible behind the moon, instead of the dramatic ink-black void in the developed masterpiece. The moon is solid white with no features. All photographers know the moon is difficult to photograph since it is many stops brighter than anything else in the night sky.

Adams was a darkroom genius. In his studio he had a custom-made enlarger on railroad tracks that had an array of individually controlled light bulbs. Compared to our modern digital photography software, developing darkroom prints was a time-consuming, painstaking process.

Adams spent days to weeks in his studio working out the exact process of burning and dodging an exposure, a choreographed dance requiring exact timing and position. Would it perturb Adams to learn that today's photographers can develop in thirty seconds in Silver Efex Pro what took him days of labor? I don't think he would be irritated. He was a technophile. He would be delighted.

I faced west toward the Jemez Mountains at sunrise while Adams had faced east toward the Sangre de Cristo Mountains at sunset. Was I doomed to be an anti-hero? I developed the images a few days later. There was something deeply peaceful about waking early, brewing coffee, and sitting at my MacBook developing images I had just taken. In the past, I always had to wait to get home before I could develop my travel images. Check another box under RV advantage.

When I developed the images in Silver Efex Pro, the similarity to Moonrise struck me. I darkened the sky and brought out highlights in the foreground. I didn't need days in a darkroom, only a few minutes with my mouse and some sliders and some control points. The final image pleased me though the source of inspiration is obvious.

We continued toward Los Alamos. I would learn later that day why there was a five-lane highway leading to this small town. We went to the Visitor's Center. Several sweet-natured elderly ladies told us what we could see and gave us maps. Around the corner we came upon the sculpture of Oppenheimer and Groves, the two principles of the Manhattan project.

J. Robert Oppenheimer was a moody, at times depressed, intense genius who did brilliant mental pirouettes in theoretical nuclear physics, astronomy, spectroscopy and quantum field theory. He delved voraciously into history, literature and philosophy. He learned Sanskrit and read the Bhagavad Gita. Had he lived longer he likely would have received a Nobel Prize for his work in gravitational physics that predicted black holes. Oppenheimer had a talent for being an inspirational instructor to younger students.

Leslie Richard Groves Jr, the commander of the Manhattan Project was a West Point graduate and engineer, who rose through the ranks by merits of accomplishment. He saved Nicaragua's water supply after a 1931 earthquake, streamlined the construction of new military training sites during the buildup to WWII and was the chief problem solver during the construction of the 5,100,000 square-foot Pentagon. After the massive effort to build the Pentagon in record time he said, "I was hoping to get to a war theater so I could find a little peace." Instead he was promoted to brigadier general and given command of the Manhattan Project. Groves commented, "Oh, that thing."

On a long train trip, Groves became impressed with Oppenheimer's broad knowledge of many disciplines and his "overweening ambition." Despite strong resistance from many due to Oppenheimer's communist party affiliations, Grove's chose Oppenheimer to lead the Los Alamos Laboratory. The rest is history. After the successful detonation of the first atomic bomb at the Trinity site, Oppenheimer said, "It worked," but later, on a television broadcast, he quoted Vishnu, "Now I am become Death, the destroyer of worlds."

Someone had dressed the statues with red plaid scarves. Barb posed between the statues. In that image she represented the connection between two men of very different backgrounds and different abilities that came together to create the most destructive weapon in mankind's history. Many of us now wish there were no nuclear weapons on earth. But there are.

We walked over to Fuller Lodge, a stately log-beam meeting hall of the former Los Alamos Ranch School that became the social activities center for the scientists and families of the Los Alamos National Laboratory. The government purchased the school and surrounding area in 1942 after deciding the site, easily defended on its mesa, was ideal for a secret facility. The Los Alamos Ranch School was an elite school modeled after the Boy Scouts of America. It combined college prep education with vigorous outdoor pursuits. Alumni include William S. Burroughs and Gore Vidal. No naked lunches were allowed.

The Lodge was the first structure on Bathtub Row, so named because the only bathtubs in town during the bomb-making days were in houses on this street. Down the street, we explored Hans Bethe's house, now a museum. Hans Bethe, a German physicist with a Jewish mother, landed at Cornell University before the war and was recruited into the theoretical division at Los Alamos. His team calculated the critical mass of uranium-235 necessary for fission in the "gadget."

Bethe won a Nobel Prize in 1967 for working out the details of the sun's nuclear energy. He became a fierce advocate of nuclear disarmament. His was a key voice in working out the 1963 Partial Test Ban Treaty and the SALT I agreement. I knew little about Bethe before walking through his house. How quickly do they fade, the names of those who contribute greatly to their generations?

Oppenheimer's house was next to Bethe's. Someone lived there. I leaned over the fence and took pictures and wondered what it would be like to live in Oppenheimer's house.

Leaving Bathtub Row, under cloudy skies that promised a shower, we toured the Bradbury Science Museum. No, it's not named after science fiction author Ray Bradbury, but rather after Norris E. Bradbury who was the second director of the Los Alamos National Laboratory. One room is dedicated to the Manhattan Project. Historic documents and photographs of the many scientists who worked on the project fill the walls.

The most enlightening exhibit was a note from President Harry S. Truman, describing that he told Stalin about the successful Trinity Bomb test in 1945. American leaders decided it was prudent to tell Stalin about the bomb to reign in his post-war ambitions. Apparently, Stalin thought he would get all of Europe as a prize of war.

Truman wrote, "He didn't realize what I was talking about." However, it's likely Stalin knew exactly what Truman was talking about since Russian spies were already stealing documents from

Los Alamos.

Another room displayed full-size models of Little Boy and Fat Man, the two atomic bombs dropped on Japan. Less emotional was the Dual-Axis Radiographic Hydrotest (DARHT) vessel, which looked like a cherry-red undersea bathysphere. This solid aluminum globe, used at the DARHT Facility, images detonations of our aging nuclear weapons using two-axis x-ray imaging. Since the banning of environmental nuclear weapon testing, this is how we do it.

The panel in front of the DARHT vessel had a lot of specific details, almost a primer on how to use it. I wondered if that information should be classified. An article from the Los Alamos Study Group in 1999 stated, "Details about the experiments, apparently to be conducted later this year, are highly classified and the fact that there is now a public discussion going on…has prompted inquiries…about a possible breach of security." Intrigue stirs the American soup. Hopefully, the museum had cleared this exhibit with the National Security Council. I saw no North Koreans lurking about.

We wanted to see the Valles Caldera, a filming location for Longmire. I envisioned photographing the epic meadow across from Walt Longmire's cabin. Apple Maps took us north through the town, around a curve and, suddenly, we were staring at an imposing boothed turnstile gate. A uniformed guard walked up to my window. "Have you been here before?" he said, evenly.

I said, "I've never been here. We're trying to get to the Valles Caldera."

He smiled. "You can drive through, but don't stop, don't take any photographs and don't get out of your car. There's nothing to see here."

We drove carefully through a block of concrete buildings housing the Los Alamos National Laboratory. The road switchbacked sharply out of the valley into a quiet, snowy winter wilderness that seemed abandoned. After miles we came to a trailhead. Nothing looked like a Longmire set. A snowman guarded the trailhead. I put a cigarette butt in his mouth and took a shot. On the return I took shots of what looked like, possibly, a caldera.

It was getting late and we wanted to see the Bandelier National Monument. A work crew delayed us. Hurry. We raced into the ranger station, hoping we still had time. A uniformed elderly woman gave us maps and told us we just had time to make it to the cliff dwellings. I asked her if the ruins here were Anasazi. Big, big mistake. The grandmotherly ranger huffed up and said, "We don't use that term. We say Ancestral Puebloans."

I had read many books about the Anasazi and I felt she was a little condescending. I said, "Yes, the term Anasazi is a Navajo word that means ancient enemy, but many authors still use the term."

She got hot. "Ancestral Puebloans is what the people that still live here use. We should respect them. They LIVE here. They built this place."

I sensed this was an important issue to her. She probably ran into folks every day saying Anasazi and she had made it her mission to stamp out that hated name. I said softly, "Yes, we should respect them." She decompressed with a wary eye.

I have an interest in Southwestern archeology. One of my apartment mates in college was an archeologist who later worked in state government and became an expert for the Arizona Land Commission. I was riveted by Craig Childs' excellent book, House of Rain. Childs traced, backpacking on foot, what may have been the evacuation route of the Anasazi population during their mysterious disappearance that more likely had been a migratory dispersal to more favorable microclimates. Childs uses the term Anasazi, but makes comment:

Ancestral Puebloans are ancestors of modern Pueblo people, and the term is steadily replacing Anasazi. It better encom-

passes an unbroken lineage of indigenous farmers from three thousand years ago to today. Whereas Anasazi refers to an archeologically defined group existing solely on the Colorado Plateau, Ancestral Puebloan is much more geographically expansive and nonspecific, depicting the entire Pueblo ancestry, whether from the Southwest or from southern Mexico.

In his late forties, my long-time friend and Geezer-founder, Jay, told his friends to call him Jack from then on. He gave no reason for this. I suspected he wanted to appear more professional in his business pursuits. However, none of us could do it. We had known him all our lives as Jay. When I had time to think, I would call him Jack, but if he called me on the phone, I reflexly said, "Hey, Jay, what's up?"

Maybe the Ancestral Puebloans could give the rest of us a little wiggle room. There are decades of research and writings using the term Anasazi. Barnes and Pendleton in their *Canyon Country Prehistoric Indians* use Anasazi. *The Historical Atlas of Native Americans* by Dr. Ian Barnes, which I got at a great bargain price at Barnes and Nobles, has an entire section labeled THE ANASAZI. *Ancient Ruins of the Southwest* by David Grant Noble, revised in 2000, uses Anasazi. There is an Anasazi State Park in southern Utah.

In Search of the Old Ones by David Roberts, copyright 1996, uses Anasazi. Roberts explains in his Author's Note:

In recent years there has been a movement among younger archeologists and some Pueblo people to substitute "Ancestral Puebloans" for "Anasazi." This book resists that nomenclature on several grounds. Whatever its faults, Anasazi has been a well-defined archeological term for almost sixty years (to distinguish that culture, for example, from the contemporary Hohokam to the south or Fremont to the north); Puebloan derives from the language of an oppressor who treated the indigenes of the South-

west far more brutally than the Navajo ever did; and, at book length, repeated again and again, "Ancestral Puebloans" is a cumbersome mouthful.

A 1974 book, *ANASAZI, Ancient People of the Rock*, with outstanding photography by the well-known David Muench and text by Donald G. Pike, also uses - well, you know.

I tried to call Jay, Jack. He was my good friend. I will also try to use the term Ancestral Puebloans particularly when addressing Native Americans, even at a Cleveland Indians game, even though it may be a cumbersome mouthful and compete with a hot dog.

We toured the highlights of Bandelier in double time, fearing the inevitable eviction by the ancient one. We passed the great kiva and climbed up the trail to the cavates, the cave rooms, dug out of volcanic tuff. In 1880, a modern, non-ancient Puebloan, Jose Montoya, led Adolph Bandelier, a Swiss-American archeologist, to this ancient Puebloan village. Bandelier lobbied to preserve the site. Woodrow Wilson agreed and declared it a National Monument. In the 1930s, the Civilian Conservation Corps built the artistic, hand-hewn visitors lodge.

We left in crepuscular light. We drove through White Rock en route to NM 502 that connects Los Alamosans to NM 285. At the junction with 502, we saw a rushing rush-hour stream of headlights streaming down from the mesa. This was the commute of the ten thousand employees of the Los Alamos complex that live in Santa Fe, hence the five lanes. Time explains all.

After an invigorating day, we floated into the welcoming lights of Santa Fe. It felt home-like. Rick's house was starting to feel home-like. However, we detected Rick was maybe feeling less home-like in his shared home.

He remarked that Waffles was staring at him when he woke up. He stared back for a long time before she looked away. I explained that when cats stare at you it means they like you. If they don't like you, they don't look at you.

We had two more days before the next storm rolled east from the Pacific, two more Seinfeld episodes before starting our homeward leg.

Barb connects two great minds

Fuller Lodge at Los Alamos Ranch School

For Ansel: *Toward the Jemez*

Moonrise Over Hernandez, New Mexico
Original contact print

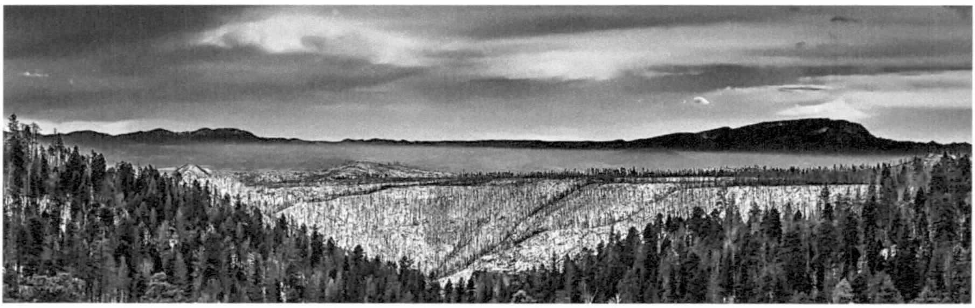

Maybe a caldera?
The Valles Caldera.

Chapter 10

Goodbye Santa Fe

A new storm bore toward Santa Fe, new snow in two days. Oregonians drive in the rain without even noticing, but I had no desire to skid out in snow at sixty-five mph in an 18,000 lb. vehicle. Rick suggested driving to the Petrified Forest before the snow hit. If it snowed, we would just hunker down, petrified, around the Petrified Forest.

I came to appreciate the Weather Channel app in planning our daily route. On the 10-day forecast page you can scroll down to the radar images, then click by half days into the future and watch the weather change in stop motion.

A huge front blossomed from California to Texas. To get home, we would have to head north under the path of the jet stream. Siskiyou Pass and Shasta Pass were possible trouble spots if there was snow. The weather was perfect in Santa Fe. Most of the snow had melted.

Rick worked at Santa Fe Community College. Many times I had called Rick at work with computer problems or just to bullshit. I wanted to see the office from which he dispatched his technical largess.

Construction of Santa Fe Community College began in 1984 and since then the campus has added seven new buildings. Oriented towards career education, Santa Fe's youth look to SFCC as the primary resource for higher education. The Santa Fe Higher Education Center, launched in 2011, offers on-line Bachelor's degrees in partnership with other four-year schools in the state.

The school is twelve miles outside downtown. We parked on campus in a crisp morning sun. Deep blue skies and a mountain ambience reminded me of NAU's campus in Flagstaff. Dusky adobe buildings seemed to grow out of the earth.

Santa Fe architecture is not just ubiquitous in Santa Fe, it is the law. By ordinance, all buildings in Santa Fe's historic district must be earth toned in the characteristic Santa Fe style. Even outside the district, those who flaunt the iconic style face the wrath of neighbors.

Rick escorted us, with running information, to the various Centers, including his department's bank of new servers. Let me tell you, these babies can crunch data, Bro. Rick's department's job is to maintain the servers that handle all the online access, e-mails and vital software that keep the college humming. No one uses books anymore! If the system goes down, the college is paralyzed. Rick is on call for after-hours problems.

There have been crises. Once someone let in a trojan virus that required the entire campus to make new passwords. The administrative analysts should be called "servers" and the servers should be called "masters."

Warm New Mexican sun flooded the hallways. I felt relaxed and content among the smiling students, youth dreaming of a future. I could learn here if I had to. The cafeteria windows framed a photographer's vision of pink adobe, the Santa Maria de la Paz church, backgrounded by the snow-capped Jemez Mountains. I could not only learn here, I could eat here. I was glad my friend worked in a place of buoyant beauty. I was also glad I was retired.

On the way home we saw an excellent movie, *Hidden Figures*, that dovetailed with the mission of equal opportunity at SFCC. After that we hung out with Waffles at Rick's house.

She's a great cat, even when staring.

When Rick walked through the door, he said, "You might want to look outside." The sky was on fire, a blaze of phosphorescent orange cloud bellies. I grabbed my gear, jumped into the rental, and sped off, trying to think of a good spot to photograph. I needed elevation, a hill. Wait a sec, Rick lived in the shadow of Museum Hill, the site of several art museums, which climbed above the surrounding neighborhood.

A right turn on Camino Lejo, the street of far distance, put me on Museum Hill. The gate was open to a parking lot at the peak of the hill. I parked, set up the tripod, and bracketed rapid fire, a desperate photon junkie. A bright orange wave of stratocumulus clouds ignited half the sky. A woman walked up and told me she was locking the gate. Thankfully I was coming down from my photon high.

The moon inched above the eastern horizon as the sun slipped away in the west. A moon cocktail after a solar feast. Thank you whoever controls nature. Several blocks away, the Arroyo de los Chamisos ran under Old Santa Fe Trail. The moon rose over Atalaya Peak.

It's difficult to expose the moon. If you stop down to get the moon's features, the rest of the image will be black, underexposed. I saw an excellent exposure of the moon over Mount Hood on Facebook by a well-known Portland photographer. Hold me he got that shot with a super high ISO. My Nikon gets too noisy over 800 ISO. I need a better camera, like an 810. Barb is gonna kill me.

I bracketed the arroyo, but every exposure had a pure white moon. However, the foreground of buff-white, softly glowing chamisos saved the day, or night. These chamisos, also called saltbush, emerged as the star models in the Arroyo de los Chamisos.

Dale Ball, who died a year ago at age ninety-one, was a retired banker from Nebraska, who fell in love with Santa Fe during a horse trip into the Pecos Wilderness. He and his wife Sylvia put together the Santa Fe Conservation Trust with the dream of establishing hiking in the lower altitude foothills accessible to the city.

Ball became an expert in easements and stitched together land, owned by various factions, into a contiguous park encompassing the peaks. He recruited Mike Wirtz, a retired trails expert for the US Forest Service, in 2000. Twenty-three miles of trails form a spaghetti of access to the peaks, Picacho and Atalaya. Thank you, Dale.

We hiked up Picacho Peak, Rick's favorite weekend hike, on a clear sunny winter day. We accessed the trailhead a half-mile down the road. The trail ended on a large mound dirt in a quarter of a mile. We called Rick. He re-oriented us. There were ice patches, but none that required crampons.

We climbed through juniper, oak and pine forest. With increasing altitude, a broad vista of the Santa Fe Valley unfurled against the sugarcoated cardiogram of the Jemez Mountains.

We ate lunch on the summit. Other hikers, trail runners, and dog lovers didn't linger long at the summit. They were regulars exercising in their backyard gym. The hike was a fitting coda to our time in Santa Fe. Tomorrow we would head into the assault of a meteorological Sturmtruppen.

Cafeteria at SFCC

Sky on Fire

Arroyo de los Chamisos

Chapter 11

Painted and Petrified

We said goodbyes after breakfast and nervously inched the Photon Bus through the labyrinth of Rick's satanic driveway. Under solid clouds, we headed west through Albuquerque on I-40. At Camping World I found a replacement for the running light I had smashed. We filled LP tanks from a guy who ran a side business out of an over-heated railroad car at the Enchanted Trails RV Park and Trading Post. Enchanted Trails had an enchanting, vintage look. Vintage trailers and cars populated most of the sites.

Low, dark clouds, Sturmtruppen, marched from the West.

The last time I had pulled into the parking lot at the Painted Desert the flag was at half-mast. I was confused until someone told me it was September 11.

The light sucked. I had to shoot the brilliant multicolored panorama of the Painted Desert in florescent blue light.

When I develop images in Lightroom, I use the white balance slider, but that can't realistically convert an overcast shot into daylight. Lightroom is a photography development and organizer program made by Adobe. I prefer it to Photoshop, also Adobe, with its confusing layers. If you don't enjoy hassling with layers, get Lightroom.

Francisco Vazquez de Coronado named this unique landscape "El Desierto Pintado" in 1540. The strong colors of the desert come from iron and manganese compounds of the Triassic

Chinle Formation. I have hiked many times in the Coronado National Forest in Arizona. You see, Francisco, those who name will be named.

The Painted Desert is a Badland. That is not necessarily a bad thing. Badlands are dry terrain eroded by wind and water, exposing softer sedimentary rocks and clay-rich soils called regolith. Other names for regolith are dirt, dust, gravel, sand and mud. Neil Armstrong's famous photograph shows his footprint in the moon's regolith. You could impress, or irritate, your neighbor by saying, "Yeah, I built my kid a regolith box."

The park road took us across a preserved segment of Old Route 66. The original Route 66 is now mostly side routes and business loops, replaced by Interstate 40. A model T artfully rusted beside this historic Mother Road that had led despondent migrating Okies from the Dust Bowl to their agricultural future in California. Route 66 wound through miles of sublime American scenery from Chicago to Los Angeles. The Mother Road gave up her scenic ghost in 1984 after completion of the final stretch of I-40 north of Williams, Arizona.

President Dwight Eisenhower signed the Interstate Highway Act in 1956. In Germany, Eisenhower discovered the Autobahn and concluded that America needed a similar high-speed road system for purposes of national security.

Years ago, Barb and I drove the Autobahn in a rented Ford Fiesta. The Fiesta's top speed was 103 mph. As a courtesy, drivers of Mercedes traveling at 150 mph would blink their lights two seconds before they roared past the grumpy Fiesta. It was no party.

Many older highways fell to the axe of The Highway Act. Some survive. Route 30, another transcontinental highway, has never been decommissioned, but only exists in short segments. You could drive from Atlantic City, New Jersey to Astoria, Oregon. In Oregon, U.S. 30 is still the main road from Portland to Astoria. It has intersections and hosts a lot of accidents.

Roland Smith, a retired professor and an accomplished photographer, was one of my favorites in The Portland Photographic Society. A WWII veteran, Roland chased Nazis in Italy sans Autobahn. He told me about old, abandoned sections of Route 30 in Oregon where one could find picturesque, decaying buildings full of ghosts.

I tried to interest the Society in a Route 30 Project, where we would photo-document all remaining segments of Route 30 and put on a grand exhibition at the Oregon Historical Society. Never happened. But Roland and a few others sent me their photos. The Historic Columbia River Highway, which runs past Crown Point and Multnomah Falls, is an old segment of Route 30. I shot some beautiful images one bright spring day on the serpentine curves of Route 30 past Mosier.

We continued south on the park road that traverses the Petrified Forest National Park. The rangers had warned us that the road closed at 5:00 pm. The free map had a taped-on message:

Park Hours 8:00 a.m. to 5:00 p.m. MST
At 5:00 p.m. you must be driving
DIRECTLY. to an exit without stopping.

Why the strict deadline? At the VA hospital where I trained, we couldn't start any surgery cases after 1:00 pm, because government employees get automatic overtime after 4:00 pm and the cases often went long. My guess is the rangers not only wanted to stop work on time, but also didn't want salivating rock hounds coming in to pilfer choice pieces of petrified wood, which would apparate with price tags in the rock shops of Holbrook.

The Petrified Forest contains fossils from the Late Triassic Period, when Arizona was a tropical rainforest in Pangaea, lingering contentedly at the equator. Dinosaurs roamed with nary a thought of asteroids or nuclear Armageddon. As time passed and continental plates moved, layers of sediment buried the ancient forest. The big logs absorbed silica from volcanic ash in the groundwater and crystallized into quartz. Humans spread into North America over the Bering Land Bridge, discovered the petrified logs, and said, "This is some cool shit!"

    Our petrified clock was running down. We bypassed many highlights along the twenty-mile drive. I noticed Newspaper Rock on the map. I read about Newspaper Rock in books about the Anasazi - I mean the Ancestral Puebloans. The Rock, full of petroglyphs, was thirty feet below the guardrail, not ideal for photos. Later I learned there was a larger Newspaper Rock at Newspaper Rock State Historic Monument in Utah. I guess this Rock was the weekly and the Utah Rock was the daily. Just in case, Rupert Murdoch has purchased both rocks.

    Luckily, we explored the Crystal Forest. The trail meandered through groves of glassy logs sparkling with buried jewels. In the wind moaned the fever dreams of rock hounds. At the parking lot, a uniformed ranger told us we were short on time and had to drive directly to the exit. He didn't say DIRECTLY, he said directly.

    We drove out of the park and turned on State Highway 180, heading through a black void into the island of lights of Holbrook, where we tucked into a full-hook-up camp, made a tasty dinner and watched NCIS on the DVD we had borrowed from the Desert Trails RV Park. We plan to return the DVD on our next trip.

    No laughing snowflakes fell, but the question floating in the night air was whether a big dump would prevent us getting to Flagstaff the next day. The weather radar showed the front sliding south from Utah. I wondered whether we could go north, outflank the storm, and make it to Canyonlands.

Petrified logs at the Petrified Desert

Waffles reminds us time is short

Artfully Rusting

What planet is this?

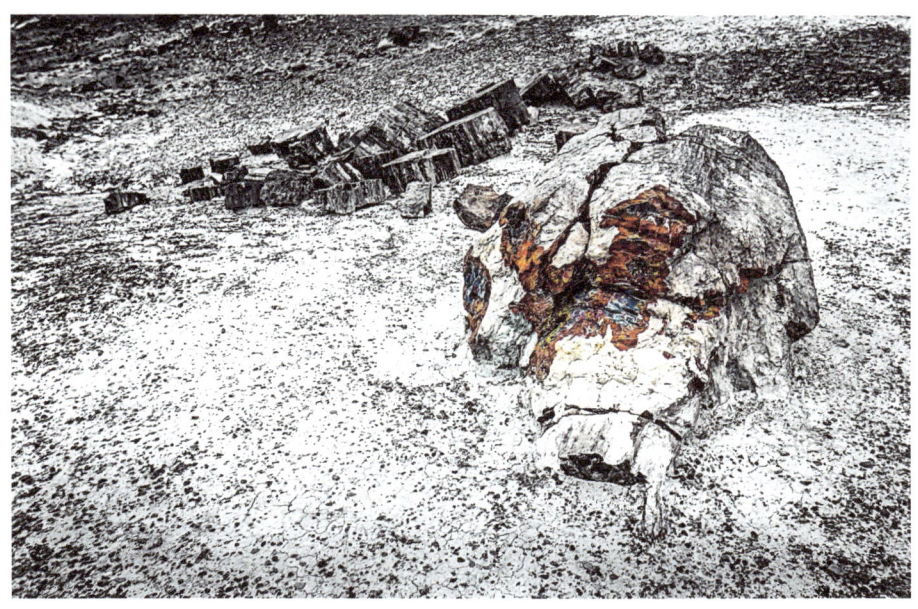

Looks Triassic to me!

CHAPTER 12

UTAH OR DEATH (VALLEY)

The morning sky in Holbrook was solid grey, not snowing or raining.

I worked on my Petrified Forest photos over coffee. After a no-cook breakfast we hit the road. The weather app showed the front moving out of Utah. I reserved a site at Canyonlands. There was a rock shop on every corner in Holbrook, no doubt owned by scheming rock hounds plotting to invade the Petrified National Forest Park under the cover of darkness.

Off the highway, a plume of white rose from tall stacks. Barb shot an iPhone picture. The Cholla Generating Station, once ranked eighth on the list of most polluting power plants, whirs out 767 megawatts. The Environment America Research and Policy Center report dropped Cholla to eighty-fifth in pollution, with 7.4 million metric tons of emissions.

My good friend and former college roommate, Bob Estes, is a retired environmental scientist, who worked on the Cholla Generating Station during his employment at Arizona Public Service. Bob informed me that the white plume is coal-firing emissions that have passed through a wet spray absorber tower prior to being routed to the stacks, reducing the sulfur dioxide and particulate matter emissions by 92 to 98 percent!

Coal plants are the top source of carbon dioxide emissions in the U.S., pumping out 1.7 billion tons in 2011. Coal plants also release sulfur dioxide, the main cause of acid rain;

nitrogen oxides, which cause ground level ozone and can burn lung tissue; particulate matter, which causes haze and exacerbates asthma; and mercury, which is toxic to brains and hearts and makes fish unsafe to eat.

Of the sixteen coal plants in Arizona, the largest is the 2,250-megawatt Navajo Generating Station, NGS, near Page. Bechtel Corporation built the $650-million, three-generator station in 1976. Electric railroad cars run coal from the Kayenta Mine. Cooling and scrubbing consumes twenty six thousand acre feet of water from Lake Powell per year. Soon after the NGS opened, the Grand Canyon became hazy. Tourists, photographers and tour operators complained. Sulfur dioxide scrubbers, installed in the 1990s, ka-chinged at $420 million.

Coal plants can reduce sulfur, nitrogen, mercury and particle pollution with scrubbers, catalytic reduction and electrostatic precipitators, but no one has come up with a solution to the massive carbon dioxide release. Natural-gas plants are cheaper and cleaner. Coal plants, burning the fossils of ancient dinosaurs, are becoming modern dinosaurs.

The biggest single producer of power in Arizona is the Palo Verde Nuclear Generating Station near Tonopah, forty-five miles west of Phoenix. Arizona's lone nuclear plant produces 3.3 gigawatts and services four million customers.

Compared to coal, nuclear power is enticing with its near-zero air pollution. However, uranium mining and transportation cause carbon pollution. Nuclear waste disposal is still an undeveloped technology with unknown future costs.

The cost of nuclear plant meltdowns is nuclear. Clean up of the Chernobyl meltdown will cost $436 billion over 30 years; the Fukushima Daiichi containment, $187 billion. British Petroleum gagged up only $100 billion for the Deepwater Horizon spill. Only! Renewable green energy production is on the rise. The answer may be blowing in the wind and shining in the sun.

Stan and Sharon were friends of ours from surgical residency days. They spent three years in Peru where Stan did surgery in wide-ranging locations. Barb and I spent a month in Peru with their family, doing surgeries and clinics and giving lectures. It was rewarding and exhausting. Experiencing the difficulties of doing medicine in a third world country was a life lesson. Years later they landed in Craig, Colorado. We visited them on our first trip in the Catalina.

In Craig, Stan made friends with miners at the Trapper Mine, a coal mine that supplied an on-site generating station. They gave us a tour. It was fascinating.

We climbed into a three-story-high dragline excavator and found a jolly, portly operator at the controls. As we entered, he bellowed, "Yabba Dabba Do." It was Fred Flintstone in the flesh. For entertainment, Fred lifted the 80-cubic-yard bucket full of dirt and rock up to its full height. He said, "Watch this," and dropped the load back into the pit. It sounded like a TNT explosion. Craig Station is fifty-fifth in national pollution ranking.

Stan introduced us to one of his patients, Dewey "Monty" Sheridan, a real cowboy who knew how to round up wild horses. Bill Moyers hosted a 1989 NPR documentary, Cowboys, featuring Monty, who lamented, "There's just not much demand for cowboys. About the only ones that's cowboys any more is some ole broken-down guys that can't do nothing else, you know." Monty took us out chasing wild horses in Sand Wash. Joshua was impressed to meet a real cowboy. Monty passed from earth at age eighty in 2013.

Rain chaperoned us into Flagstaff. The roads were clear, but there were five-foot mounds of snow in the parking lots. I attended Northern Arizona University in Flagstaff for two years. One day, at the end of a two-hundred-inch snow season, the sun came out and there was no wind. Everyone was running around in T-shirts and shorts. I checked the temperature out of curiosity. It was thirty-two degrees Fahrenheit. What is warm to an Inuit, is freezing to a Panamanian.

We exited I-40 and crossed Historic Route 66, then up Highway 89. Soon there was snow on either side of the highway. After ten miles, the snow was covering the entire road. We made a nervous U-turn through a median gap and headed south. I wanted to explore southern Utah, but boo-hoo for me. Another time. Death Valley was an alternative. Does it ever snow in Death Valley?

Historic Route 66, the I-40 business loop, merged back into the interstate west of town. The road smoothed out after some bumpy miles. We dropped off the Colorado Plateau as we emerged from the Kaibab National Forest, heading toward Seligman.

Three landscapes divide Arizona: Basin and Range, Colorado Plateau and Transition Zone (the Mogollon Rim). The southern and western areas of the state, sites of the main population centers, are in the Basin and Range Province, composed of north-south trending sky island mountain ranges with intervening alluvial basins. Most geologist agree that stretching and thinning of the lithosphere caused fault blocks to rise as ranges, with sinking of the intervening basins, known as horst and graben formation.

Northern Arizona, along with adjacent areas of Utah, Colorado and New Mexico, lies on the Colorado Plateau, which rose to its mile-plus elevation during the Laramide Orogeny in the late Cretaceous, 80 million years ago. Instead of rising as mountains, as in the Rockies, the Plateau, with a thicker, stronger crust, ascended as a solid block. Later, tilting of the Plateau caused drainages, such as the Colorado River, to cut canyons into the stacked layers of strata that date back to the pre-Cambrian. The Grand Canyon is a geologic infant, only five million years old.

I've had good times in the Canyon. In 1974, a group of us college kids on spring break packed into Havasupai Creek, a tributary of the Colorado River. Here turquoise-colored waters cascade over a series of falls. One senses this is Eden, a milk-blue dream rushing over a thousand travertine bathtubs.

No one had the foresight to make reservations with the Supai tribe. The usual route is the mule trail from Haulapai Hilltop. We heard about an old Indian trail that cut through the mesa. We found it. In places, we passed our packs down a human chain. Scree slopes became dusty ski slopes. After dark, we crept through the village, silent as Indians, and set up camp below Mooney Falls.

The next day, a Supai ranger, Wayne, walked into our camp and told us we had to leave. We pleaded that we were just nice college kids on spring break. He sympathized and told us he would discuss our request with the tribal council.

Instead of waiting for the tribe's decision, we hiked further downstream. This was the dumbest of the options we came up with. The next morning, we woke to the sound of helicopters descending, like Rambo, on our camp. Park rangers gave us a stern talking to, followed by a court summons, and ordered us to march out and present ourselves to the court in Williams. The judge charged each of us twenty-five dollars, which is less than current camping fees.

Years later, I met the sister of Wayne, the Supai Ranger, at the Phoenix Indian Hospital. I asked her how Wayne was doing. She said, "He's dead!" Shocked, I asked her how. "Wife killed him." I told the sister I was very sorry as Wayne had been nice to us.

Past Seligman, mountain ranges shivered in the distance, the Aquarius Mountains and the Hualapai Mountains. We were back in Basin and Range country. A great wall of clouds slid down the Haulapais.

Siri gave us directions to the park in Kingman. She told us to turn on Andy Devine Avenue. Andy Devine! Yes, Andy grew up in Kingman. They named an avenue after him and also have Andy Devine Days with a parade and a rodeo.

Those of us of the right age grew up hearing Andy's

trademark high-pitched gravelly voice in many cowboy movies. "Sheriff, they was a comin and they was a hootin and a hollerin." Mr. Devine claimed his vocal tone resulted from a childhood accident with a kitchen rod. Some question that. When asked if he had nodes on his vocal cords, he replied, "I've got the same nodes as Bing Crosby, but his are in tune." Andy Devine performed serious roles in his four-hundred movie career, but he was most beloved as the comic sidekick in his westerns.

We buttoned down at our park. The radar painted a hole in the giant marching storm, right over Death Valley. Death Valley was life! We sought life in the sun in Death Valley.

Cholla Generating Station

Chapter 13

Death Valley Daze and the Harvest of Photons

The morning sky above Kingman threatened to clear.

While cleaning the cat box, a wild-eyed park maintenance man in coveralls drove up in his golf cart. The conversation veered into him telling me about a large canyon in Antarctica where the government had a secret lair. I later found out there is a massive canyon larger than the Grand Canyon under the ice in Princess Elizabeth Land, discovered by radio-wave imaging. I could neither confirm nor deny the story of the secret lair.

A man came by walking dogs. I patted the beautiful golden retriever. He remarked, "She's retarded." He repeated that descriptor several times during the conversation. Loquacious, he was a retired cop, a specialist in accident-site recreation, scheduled to give a two-week course in Hawaii. When he talked about himself, he raised his eyebrows. Ahaa!

Holding forth, he told me many details about the purchase of his new toy hauler Fifth Wheel and the maddening discovery that his Harley was too long for the trailer, but his wife's Harley fit. He didn't ask me any questions, so I didn't tell him I was on classified CIA business investigating secret lairs in Antarctica.

With our mentally superior cat perched on the dashboard, we headed to Death Valley. In Las Vegas, Siri led us off I-215 through concrete-block neighborhoods before connecting us to

NV 160. We made it through Pahrump without being drawn into the magnet of casinos or that ranch where they grow chickens.

I looked forward to a good harvest of photons in Death Valley. The term, harvesting photons, may be erudite, but it more accurately describes image creation than the word, photography. Phos is the Greek word for light. Photograph literally means "written with light." Camera sensors absorb, or harvest, photons, rather than write with them

The goal of photography is to make a record of the flow of photons coming from a defined area over a defined amount of time. Photons! That's an itch that's hard to scratch. What are photons? How can something that has zero mass be anything?

The best of human minds have tried to achieve photonic enlightenment. Both wave and particle, photons have various frequencies, but can occupy a certain position with a certain momentum. Thanks to Heisenberg's Uncertainty Principle, we can't measure simultaneously both position and momentum. Per Albert Einstein, photons have energy in discrete packages, or quanta. Photons may not be an actual thing, but rather carriers of the electromagnetic force. In the Standard Model of physics, photons are gauge bosons.

That gives me an idea. I'm going back to see the ranger at Bandelier National Monument, the one that lectured me about Anasazi, and wait until she might have to say the word "light." Then I'll mention that physicists prefer the term "gauge boson" and since they're doing all the hard work that may allow us to one day escape our dying planet we should respect their nomenclature. No, I won't do that. But I can dream.

We photographers are most thankful that photons can pull off the photoelectric effect. A photon can transfer its energy to something else, like an atom or a molecule. In our digital camera sensors, silicon diodes absorb photons. A current of electrons diffuses through the diode in proportion to the number of photons hitting the sensor. Camera sensors have cavities, called wells, or photosites, that trap photons. Each well corresponds to a pixel. Pixels are the little rectangles of color that make the images we so love.

Camera consumers, including myself, focus on megapixels. More megapixels resolve a higher resolution image. Few consumers consider the size of the wells, which profoundly affects image quality. A larger well can gather more photons over a specific amount of time. If you have a camera with a lot of megapixels, but with smaller wells, the low-light sensitivity will not be as good.

Ninety three photons land on a square micrometer during a 1/60 second exposure from a full moon. Full sunlight blasts 7.4 million photons on the same area. If we want to shoot starlight, or the moon, we want big wells. Wells on my Nikon sensor are 35.4 square microns, each harvesting 3,300 photons during that 1/60 second exposure of the moon.

My Nikon has 24.3 million wells. The Nikon D810 that I covet if I can get around Barb, has 36.3 million wells, but the well size, the area of a single photosite, is smaller at 23.7 square microns. The D810 has better resolution, but the D600, now called the D610, has better low light sensitivity and dynamic range.

The Canon 5DS R has a whopping 50.3 megapixels. Since the Canon's sensor size is the same as my Nikon's, it must fit more megapixels into the same area. So, the Canon has smaller individual wells, less than half the size of the Nikon's wells.

Compared to either the Nikon D810 or the Canon 5DS R, the Nikon D600, with its larger wells, has less noise at high ISO and better dynamic range, though less resolution. I still want an upgrade. DPReview haunts my email like the sirens singing to Homer. My best choice is to delay any new camera purchase until the next generation and hide from the inevitable spousal darts. "What are you buying now!"

Camera nerds!

Where were we?

The sky was blue at Zabriskie Point just inside the entrance to Death Valley. This is one of those locations where it's impossible to take a bad photograph. Zabriskie Point, a colorful badland on the west slope of the Amargosa Range, is part of the Furnace Creek Formation. Its ochre colors come from mud, gravel and ash sediments, deposited in ancient Lake Manly over the past few million years.

It's a great place to photograph. It was also, thought the magnificently-named Italian director, Michelangelo Antonioni, a great place to film an erotic sex scene for a movie. Zabriskie Point is a 1970 film, co-written by Sam Shepard and others, that Antonioni hoped would become a counter-culture classic like *Easy Rider*.

An existential-minded student flees a bloody campus protest, steals a Cessna, and flies to Zabriskie Point, where he melds with a beautiful woman in a dusty orgy. Critics, including Roger Ebert, panned the film, which bombed. Production costs were $7 million; domestic receipts were only $900,000.

The Department of Justice investigated whether the producers violated the Mann Act, but no one was transported across state lines and the sex was fake movie sex. The best qualities of the film were the title and the soundtrack that featured Pink Floyd, Jerry Garcia, the Youngbloods, the Rolling Stones, John Fahey, Patti Page and Roy Orbison. It might have been better as a concert. Antonioni made many notable films, including , and received an Honorary Academy Award, presented by Jack Nicholson the star of *Easy Rider*.

I saw no writhing bodies as I shot Zabriskie in late afternoon light. I shot a panorama, but the guy on the edge moved during the set and in the pano he had no neck. It's good to put people, or objects of familiar dimension, in the foreground of landscape photographs to give a sense of true dimension.

We went to Furnace Creek and paid for two nights in the

no-hook-up campground. It was the worst camp of the trip, rock-strewn, viewless, crowded, with barking dogs and generators screeching into the night.

Zabriskie Point

Chapter 14

Ghosts and UFOs

I have accumulated a pet menagerie of songbirds in my yard. I like to sit in a rocking chair at a spot under my pin oaks that overlooks my pond, home to some resident mallards and an ever-stalking great blue heron. Last spring, a Song Sparrow showed up. He would perch on a rhododendron and sing his full mating song. I responded a few times using my Peterson app (Birds of North America). He found a mate and built a nest in a nearby cottonwood. I feared he would migrate during winter, but he was always there. This spring a Spotted Towhee joined him, sometimes perched on a different rhododendron, sometimes on the same, close to the Song Sparrow. A pair of Black-Capped Chickadees and a Dark-eyed Junco joined the menagerie. I played the Junco's song on my Peterson and he flew over and perched six feet away. A chipmunk has joined the crowd, munching on seeds that spill out of the feeder. I have never, in thirty years, seen a chipmunk in western Oregon.

We woke before sunrise and made tracks to Badwater Basin. I had researched online for prime photography sites (https://jamesb.com). Nice thing that online. Thanks to James Brandon.

The rising sun was behind the Amargosas when we reached the turnoff to Devil's Golf Course. I saw no golf course.

Where is this golf course? There was no golf course, of course, but there was a great pano of mist lingering over the valley floor.

There were only a few cars at the Badwater parking lot, plenty of room for the Photon Bus. The shot was out of a dream. The moon floated over the Panamint Mountains in an ink-blue sky. Without recent rain, the iconic salt hexagonals had transitioned into shag carpet. No matter, this was still an alien dream landscape.

It was also two hundred eighty-two feet below sea level, the lowest spot in North America. I didn't feel low. I felt high. A sign on the cliff face demarcated sea level. Crunching through a mile of salt, I took two hundred thirty-five exposures. Barb made pancakes. We ate in the Bus, watching the shadow of the Amargosas creep toward us across a valley of white crystals. I give this restaurant four stars.

After breakfast, we headed to Mesquite Flats Sand Dunes, sandwiched between the Funeral Mountains and the Cottonwood Mountains. These dunes, not the largest in Death Valley, were the most accessible, good enough for George Lucas to film some *Star Wars* scenes.

We sifted into the dunes. A line of marching ant-people climbed up Star Dune, the largest, so we veered south. One thing I have learned is that you never know which shot will be the money shot. Through the viewfinder, you see only a small scene. Forget looking at the LED live view screen in full sunlight. I shoot lots of exposures, kind of like trout fishing where you cast into any water that might be productive.

We hiked a mile out and back. The Funeral Mountains made a dramatic background for the dunes. I thought there might be a money shot in the SD card. We drove a short distance to Stovepipe Wells. Compared to Furnace Creek, Stovepipe felt like a luxury resort, clean with few loitering tourists and no screaming kids. The general store sold happy, kitschy curios to weary prospectors. I'm a sucker for curios. Perhaps we could throw Furnace Creek down a stovepipe? I walked into the office and asked if there were any full-hook-up sites available. Hey Hosanna, there was one spot left.

We parked in our site with full hookups. Hook me up, baby. To the north, shimmered a Zen-inducing mind rush of sun-drenched alluvial bliss. Joyful vibes. Lunch and a glass of wine in a camp chair made me forget about the Furnace Creek camp. After a nap, we were ready to head through Daylight Pass into the ghost town of Rhyolite.

It's not a good idea to name your town after a rock or a mineral. Towns with such names collapse. In Arizona: Black Diamond, Chloride, Copper Creek, Goldfield, Goldroad, Oro Blanco, Oroville, and Ruby all bit the alluvial dust. In Nevada: Bullionville, Coaldale, Gold Acres, Gold Butte, Gold Center, Gold Point, Goldfield, Quartz Mountain, Rhyolite, Ruby Hill, Silver Canyon, and Sulphur all saw their municipal skarn mineralization peter out.

Some rock towns have survived. Boulder is doing well. Moscow, named after muscovite, used in medieval times to make Muscovy glass, is hanging in there. It might be a better bet to name your town after a hope-inspiring religious symbol, like Los Angeles or San Francisco or Santa Fe.

In 1907, Rhyolite, Nevada, founded during the gold rush of the Bullfrog Mining District, had a population of four thousand. Charles M. Schwab bought the largest of the mines, the Montgomery Shoshone Mine. Bad investment!

Schwab underwrote a massive municipal upgrade of Rhyolite, including electric lights, water mains, telephones, newspapers, schools, an opera house, a public swimming pool and, of course, a stock exchange. These amenities were worth millions in current currency values. Schwab persuaded three railroads to build service lines to the town. There were fifty saloons and two churches, the typical gold-town ratio.

Investors got nervous and ordered an independent inspection by a mining engineer. The inspection determined the high-grade ore was almost gone. The 1906 San Francisco (not named after a rock) earthquake diverted venture capital away from mining and the Financial Panic of 1907 swept away the last crumbs of investment bread.

Rhyolite disintegrated and, by 1920, only fourteen, likely very colorful, individuals remained. The ghost town, Rhyolite, became a tourist stop and occasional movie set. It's unlikely you will find a picture of Rhyolite on the walls of any Charles Schwab investment office.

James Brandon's photography website had an admirable night shot of the old bank in Rhyolite. I wanted my own. We nudged the Photon Bus up Daylight Pass, 3,800 feet above our sea-level camp. We arrived at sunset. The ghost town was deserted. Or was it? I shot the sunset, using ghost buildings as foreground.

I made a rookie mistake. Stars, as you might think, do not focus at infinity. Stars focus slightly below infinity. Since my autofocus doesn't work well at night, I focus, before twilight, on a distant object, then turn off the autofocus. In the consummation of the vibrating samsara that is Rhyolite, I forgot to set my focus.

As the stars blinked into view, a frigid, biting katabatic wind descended. Barb and Waffles stayed in the Photon Bus while I braved the cold. I immobilized my tripod with my full body weight. Shuffling sounds creaked in the ruins. Maybe the wind?

Back at Stovepipe Springs, I shot long exposures of the Milky Way. It was then I realized my mistake. Since I couldn't autofocus in the dark, I manually edged the focus back from infinity. Cursing, I figured the Rhyolite shoot was shot. Shit!

The next morning I discovered something interesting in the Rhyolite shots, a strange shape among the stars over the old bank where Mr. Schwab's deposits rotted. At Venus, a horizontal string of lights hovered, an odd dome structure on top. I thought it might have been camera shake, but none of the other stars showed this effect. My pulse quickened. I had photographed a UFO!

All my life I've wanted to see a UFO. I grew up reading the old science fiction authors, Ray Bradbury, Isaac Asimov, Robert Heinlein and Lester del Rey. I had never seen a UFO, but now I had photographed one! An internet search discovered similar UFOs. Therefore, I had indisputable evidence I had snagged a genuine alien craft peering down at me, no doubt wondering what a member of an unfathomable species was doing in a dead town in a cold wind looking at the stars.

Go ahead. Transport me! I dare you. Call Al Gore! Call Jerry Brown! Call President Trump! No, don't call Trump.

We would have liked to have stayed several more days in Death Valley, this warm, photo-giving oasis, but there were storms gearing up in the Pacific. We needed to get through the passes between snows.

Our son texted he was not going back to college in Eugene. He had come home over Christmas break. A huge snow storm clamped down on Portland, where, apparently, lots of people were staying at our house, sledding and snowballing and doing what I did at that age. I figured the party was just too good, and he didn't want to give it up. We talked. He gave me a lot of weak, but fluent, excuses why college was a waste of his time. I told him his other choice was to move home and get a job. He didn't like that, so he agreed to go back to school.

After that conversation, my psychological tires deflated. I felt the need to head home and be available. I had assumed after I retired, I would never be on-call again. Wrong.

Badwater Basin. Not bad!

Mesquite Flats Sand Dunes

Rhyolite Sunset

UFO hovers over Charles Schwab's Bank

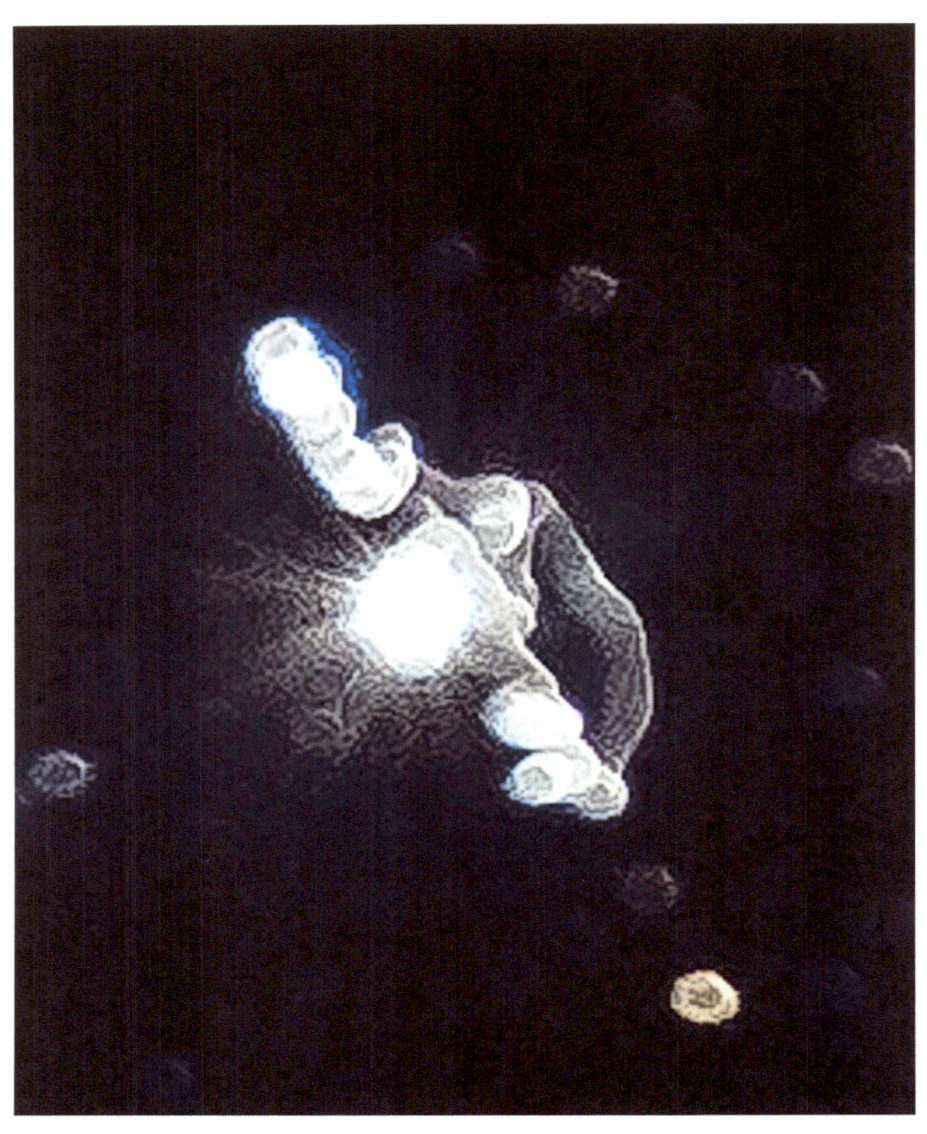

Blow-up of UFO

CHAPTER 15

WRONG TURN, RIGHT MOVE

Zen Driving is driving around aimlessly. When you stop, there you are. I like to do Zen Photography. I cruise into an unknown area and drive, or walk, around looking for shots. Sometimes I find good shots, sometimes not. Sometimes I high-ground my Toyota Tacoma in the snow en route to Bagby Hot Springs and have to pay a lot of money to have a Sno-Cat come tow me out.

As I had been doing for the latter half of the trip, I looked at a map after breakfast and decided how far I wanted to drive. I Googled RV parks in that area, looked at pictures and reviews, then called and reserved a spot. If you tried to do that kind of last-minute booking in high summer season you would run into a lot of full parks. But this was January. I booked a spot in Tehachapi at the Mountain Valley RV Park. It had the best name. I like mountains and I like valleys.

We had a bacon-and-eggs breakfast. Waffles had her special treats, which always makes her tail stand up and quiver. We could have spent another week or two exploring Death Valley, but a vague undercurrent of urgency was germinating, a triple threat of storms, snow and son.

We lumbered away from our happy camp westward on CA 190, past Emigrant Canyon, and up the curving climb of Towne Pass. The descent after the hump of the Panamint Mountains was steep. Even with the engine braking I was using the brakes before every curve. I pulled over for some brake cooling, then glided down into the Panamint Valley, the little sister of Death Valley. It was at the junction of CA 178, known as the Trona-Wildrose Road, that the legacy of Edsger Wybe Dijkstra made the next decision on our route.

At the heart of any navigation system lies an algorithm that computes the answer to the "shortest path problem," how to get from point A to point B in the shortest distance or, in more sophisticated algorithms, how to get there in the shortest time.

Edsger Dijkstra (1930-2002), a pioneering Dutch computer scientist, spent the last fifteen years of his career as a chaired professor at the University of Texas in Austin. He contributed many groundbreaking concepts to computer science, including the optimization of garbage collection. He argued against the GOTO statement in basic programming, which led to the revolution of structured programming. Dijkstra worked out the shortest-path algorithm without resorting to pen and paper while riding on a train to Leiden. Einstein, similarly, did some of his best work on train rides.

Dijkstra's algorithm calculates the shortest path through an array of intersections, or nodes, using paths of different weights. In navigation algorithms, pathways are called edges and weights can be multifactorial, incorporating distance, time, traffic conditions, road conditions, etc.

Dijkstra's algorithm is greedy; it takes up a lot of RAM, and time, calculating long complex routes. In 1968, three scientists working on an artificial intelligence project known as "Shakey the Robot," created a faster algorithm, known as A $*$ (A-star), that calculates the "least cost" of paths and uses a heuristic that estimates the cost of upcoming, uncalculated paths and prioritizes which paths to explore.

I maintain neither Apple Maps nor Google Maps has worked out what I call the Shitty Road Conundrum. No navigation app has ever asked me what vehicle I was driving. There is no way to instruct the app that I'm driving in a VERY LOUD vehicle that AMPLIFIES the sound of a rough road. Can you hear me now? Of course you can't. I suspect our instruction to turn onto a two-lane, sine-wave-surfaced rattle-fest, instead of continuing straight to the glassy four-lane of U.S. Route 395, was an act of revenge from none other than Shakey the Robot himself.

Though the road vibrations were maddening, the photonic vibrations coming from the Panamints were exquisite. We passed less than a handful of other vehicles shaking our way down the valley and over a narrow, harrowing hairpin pass. Just before our teeth fell out we pulled into the mercy of a rest stop in the factory town of Trona, home of the Searles Valley Minerals chemical plant. Multiple posters, none of which shook or rattled, told us all about Trona.

Trona is not only the name of the town, but also the name of a mineral that is the primary source of sodium carbonate in the United States. They could have named the town, trisodium hydrogendicarbonate dihydrate, but it wouldn't have changed anything. Trona came to life in 1913 to house the miners that harvested borax out of Searles Dry Lake. The company paid the miners in scrip that was only good at company stores.

The town, if not the miners, enjoyed a boom when Trona saved our national bacon during WWI. We needed potassium to make gunpowder, and the Kaiser had placed the usual European sources of potash under embargo. Soda ash, which comes from trona, is found in a wide variety of manufactured goods such as the sulfur scrubbers used in coal generating plants.

Once a year, the citizens have a festival where everyone digs through a huge pile of mud from the lakebed looking for a beautiful, golden mineral called hanksite. The town folk discard their clothes because the mud-soaked clothe dries into a petrified state. A picture showed a pair of jeans standing all on its own, which I suspect might do well at a Christie's auction.

We fired Siri and used our road atlas to map the rest of

the drive. CA 14 took us through the stately cliffs of Red Rock State Park, then a short run on CA 58 brought us to Tehachapi. We passed a huge solar installation, the Beacon 1. We found Mountain Valley next to a small airport popular with gliders. The pleasant woman who checked us in told us not to wander into the fields next to the park as they were emergency landing strips. When I asked, she did not remember seeing anyone land there.

From our camping spot, I saw a row of white, three-bladed wind turbines lazily rotating. This was the western terminus of the Tehachapi Pass Wind Farm, one of the first utility-scale wind farms built in the U.S. The three-blade models were large Danish-built, three megawatt turbines. Older two-blade models generate only kilowatts. One of our Boy-Scout-parent friends does high-angle repair on wind turbines. In conversation, he communicated a personal vendetta against the early model, piece of crap, turbines.

The Tehachapi Pass Wind Farm, at 690 MW, is little brother to the largest wind farm in the state, Alta Wind Energy Center (1,548 MW), located just over the pass, toward Mojave. Mountain passes and rivers are high wind sites. The San Gorgonio Pass Wind Farm that we had driven through on the rainy drive to Palm Springs, comes in at number three with 619 MW.

Wind, the earth's way of moving heat around, is a form of solar energy. The Mojave Desert, part of the sun-belt of intense solar radiation that extends across the southwestern U.S. into Texas, has lots of heat and lots of wind. It's a good place to harvest photons because there are a lot of them.

These days, solar cells are everywhere, the flat black modules on our rooftops, on space stations or the solar lights in our garden pathways. Photovoltaic cells work the same way as the sensors in our DSLR cameras. Photons bump up the energy of electrons from the emitter region of a silicon diode into an absorber region, creating a separation of positive and negative charges, and thus current. Newer generation solar cells may use non-silicon, thin-film diode materials, such as gallium-arsenic or cadmium-technetium, which give higher efficiency.

The physics of solar cells is densely complex. Here's how Jeffery L. Gray, Professor of Electrical and Computer Engineering at Purdue University, describes a solar cell, using his most benign, simplistic language:

A solar cell is simply a pn-junction diode consisting of two quasi-neutral regions on either side of a depletion region with an electrical contact made to each quasi-neutral region. Typically, the more heavily doped quasi-neutral region is called the emitter and the more lightly doped region is called the base…often referred to as the absorber region.

Simple. Does anyone else feel lightly doped? Multi-junction solar cells use several layers of diode material to catch more photons. The early solar cells of the 1970s had under ten percent efficiency. A German company, Fraunhofer ISE, made a four-junction cell that uses concentrated solar light with a laboratory-measured efficiency of forty-six percent.

Concentrated solar uses lenses, similar to the Fresnel lenses we like to photograph on lighthouses, to increase the light intensity. Thermal solar uses reflected sunlight to capture heat that runs a steam generator. Trough systems reflect heat into a pipe running along the focal point of the trough. Power Towers, popularized as a film location in the movie Sahara, reflect sunlight from a surrounding circular array of mirrors aimed at a sizzling, 750° F, single point. Yowza!

Solar and wind power are approaching grid parity, meaning they can cost the same or less than other power sources, such has coal, natural gas or hydropower. In the solar industry there is a Swanson's Law, similar to the Moore's Law that told us we would all have incredible computer speed in our homes. Swanson's Law states that with every doubling of cumulative production of solar panels there will be a twenty percent reduction in cost. The price of silicon photovoltaic cells has dropped from $76.67 per watt in 1977 to $0.36 per watt in 2014.

So answer me this. Why has every new DSLR camera with sensors similar to solar cells cost me more than the one before? Do we need new trade agreements with countries that make cameras to bring down the cost? Where is my photonic grid parity?

If you look at the National Renewable Energy Laboratory wind map of the U.S., you see a wide zone of purple and red, high wind speed, in the great plains of middle America and narrower stripes along both coasts. In the western states there is a spider-web of high winds in canyons and mountain passes that looks almost insignificant compared to the plains or the coasts.

This may explain why the states with the most installed wind power are those in the "great horn" of middle America. Texas can boast the most wind power by far at 20,321 MW. Texans like to boast. All that boasting will add to the free Canadian imported wind that rips through middle America. Iowa and Oklahoma, in the Great Plains, have more wind farms installed than in the greater acreage of California.

The evening winds coming through Tehachapi Pass were light at our pleasant camp site. Snow was forecast for tomorrow. We made plans to rise early and head for the coast. It turned out to be an interesting route.

On the Trona-Wildrose Road.
Good photonic vibrations.

CHAPTER 16

WELL OILED MACHINE

We bought supplies at the Kingdom of the Reliable Parking Lot, Walmart, in Bakersfield. Years ago, driving back from Palm Springs, my brother and I pulled over in Bakersfield for a golf break. It was one of the roughest courses I've ever seen, with rock-hard ground and scarce grass. However, as they say, it was golf. The only good thing about the course was my brother getting his first eagle on a par five.

In the same spirit as Andy Devine Avenue in Kingman, Bakersfield has honored two favorite sons. If Buck Owens Boulevard didn't change its name into Airport Drive on the other side of Highway 99, it would intersect with Merle Haggard Drive.

Buck and Merle intersected in life by creating the Bakersfield Sound. *Buck Owens and the Buckaroos* and *Merle Haggard and the Strangers* used Fender Telecasters, picked with energetic twang, drums, fiddles and pedal steel to back their muscular vocals. Their style was a left turn and a holler away from the orchestral-backed Nashville sound of the 50s and 60s.

I saw Merle Haggard when he opened for Bob Dylan. Merle confessed he did smoke marijuana in Muskogee. In his later years Merle mellowed from the hard-guy, anti-hippie, fightin-side-of-me image of his youth. Something had made him mellow. The Bakersfield Sound influenced a lot of younger musicians like Dwight Yoakam, Grateful Dead, Creedence Clearwater Revival, Byrds and many others. Good work Merle, Buck. May your boulevards be free of potholes.

There are four major highways running north to south in California, but they don't want to make it easy to drive across the state transversely. I found that out in the past when we cut across from CA 395 to I-5 on Highway 108 over the spine of the Sierra Nevada, straining in first gear up miles of fifteen-degree roads.

On the big atlas map, Highway 58 looked like it would get us to our destination, Morro Bay, but after the town of Buttonwillow the straight road morphed into irregular zigzags across the San Joaquin Valley and up over the coastal Diablo Range. It seemed odd the road would not be arrow straight across the valley.

Oh well. We headed west on Highway 58, which led through farmlands and suburban neighborhoods. Just before the town of McKittrick, the highway morphed into tight hairpins. Heavy trucks belched like dinosaurs on an octopus of dirt roads. I wondered if it would be like this for the next hundred miles. At the junction in McKittrick, we pulled over and studied the map. We could cut up Highway 33 to 46. It looked straighter.

Not everyone loves deserts. Scions of the lush, green Pacific Northwest, where I live, complain the desert looks brown and dead. Spend time among the cacti, I say to my provincial friends. Deserts are beautiful and filled with life. The Mojave, the Sonoran, the Chihuahuan all have their particular charms. I unwind when I can see hundreds of miles to distant mountains.

T. S. Elliot could have received inspiration from the desert tableau we witnessed through the ample windshield of the Photon Bus. Just off the roadside, a horde of giant metal grasshoppers penetrated the lifeless, flat wasteland, erotically sucking black earth-juice in perpetual rhythm. We floated through endless miles of thousands of yellow-headed pumpjacks, bisected by gleaming silver pipelines that made curious vertical loops. This was the South Belridge Oil Field, one of many massive oil fields in Kern County, which produces eighty percent of California's oil from 43,568 active wells.

The oil and gas under Kern County traveled through faults from the source rock of the Miocene shale in the Monterey Formation, which extends under the western half of California from San Francisco to Los Angeles, including substantial offshore areas. A fault, the San Andreas, runs through it. The Monterey shale is thicker than most other productive oil shales, an oilman's pump dream. But there is a problem.

Most productive tight-oil shale formations in North America, like the Bakken Shale, which has brought a billion-dollar state surplus to North Dakota, or the Barnett Shale, which lies under the house I grew up in, in Fort Worth, form in orderly horizontal layers, like a cake, cooked in the seismically quiet craton of the North American Plate. A cake served on a plate. The Monterey Formation, at the active edge of the plate, is formed more like if a three-year-old was allowed to attack his layered birthday cake while his friends egged him on.

The term, unconventional play, applies to both the three-year-old's cake mongering and the oil fields of the Monterey Shale. A petroleum play, in geology speak, is a community of oil reserves that live in the same set of structural circumstances. Due to the disrupted play, horizontal drilling and hydraulic fracturing, called fracking, don't work as well in the Monterey Formation.

In 2011 the US Energy Information Administration, EIA, issued a report that the Monterey Shale Formation contained 15.4 billion barrels of oil, more than half the recoverable shale oil in the United States. Seeing successful fracking elsewhere, California oil companies went on a bidding spree for leases and sunk exploratory wells in search of the black gold. Yeeha!

The race was on. It was Sutter's Mill all over again except blacker and greasier. A study from the University of Southern California, in 2013, estimated that hydraulic fracturing, if successful in California, could generate 2.8 million jobs and lubricate state tax collections by $24.6 billion.

Then, J. David Hughes, a Canadian geoscientist and Fellow of the Post Carbon Institute, put a pin in the unnatural gas balloon. His report, entitled *Drill Baby Drill*, argued that the EIA's estimate was over-inflated by ninety percent. In the meantime, oil failed to gush up to expectations from the wrecked-layer-cake shale. The EIA meekly dropped its estimate to 600 million barrels and ran out the door, saying it had double-parked. Then the USGS, in 2015, calculating reserves based on known success rates in two study areas in Kern County, downgraded its previous estimate of recoverable reserves by ninety-six percent to 21 million barrels of oil and 27 billion cubic feet of gas.

During this slide of industrial corporate hope, fracking became a fractious issue in California. Hydraulic fracturing injects large volumes of water and sand at pressures up to 15,000 psi, along with chemicals to make water "slick," through wellbores into tight-oil shales or sands. The sand, called proppant, props open microfactures, allowing seepage of oil and gas to the well's pipes. High-volume hydraulic fracturing, called massive fracking, uses massive volumes of proppant, at least 136 metric tons per well.

Citizens of a state that has suffered a multi-year, severe drought may be unhappy that their lawn or golf-course or drinking water has been diverted to fossil fuel extraction. Water that comes out of the well, brine, is laced with toxic chemicals and must be recycled or disposed of by injection into deep Class II wells. Toxins and methane gas can get into groundwater either by underground connections, a problem in the shallow wells of the Monterey, or spills of fracking fluid. The 2010 documentary, *Gasland*, by Josh Fox, showed home-owner's faucets flaring like cigarette lighters.

Shale gas production in the U.S. has risen from 5 billion cubic feet per day in 2007 to over 40 billion cubic feet per day, mostly from nine major formations. A graph of earthquake frequency, greater than magnitude 3.0, in central and eastern U.S. shows an abrupt, steep rise in the frequency of quakes starting in 2010, from a historic average of twenty-four per year to three hundred eighteen per year. The 2016 Pawnee earthquake in Oklahoma broke the state record with a 5.8 magnitude temblor felt over an area greater than a Sooners-Longhorn stadium stomp.

The USGS concluded, in its National Seismic Hazard Map study, that high-pressure, underground injection of oil drilling wastewater, the bulk of which is non-fracking wastewater, caused the new swarms of earthquakes. Californians look at this and say, "We already have enough earthquakes, thank you." Oregonians look at Californians and say, "We already have enough Californians."

On September 20, 2013, California passed Senate Bill 4, sponsored by State Senator Fran Pavley, the "mother of California climate change policy." SB4 requires permitting, reporting and monitoring of all hydraulic fracturing and acidizing well stimulations. Senator Pavley, a former middle school teacher, also authored SB32, which mandates a forty percent reduction in greenhouse gas emissions by 2030.

A subsequent bill, SB1132, which called for a statewide moratorium on fracking and evaluation of potential groundwater contamination, was defeated. Some think the $15 million spent by the oil industry may have been a factor. To date, six California counties, including Monterey County, the fourth-largest oil producer, have passed measures to ban fracking.

It seemed like we would never get through the oil fields. We were stuck in an Armageddon time loop. The imagery had a strange, dark hold on me. I wasn't thinking about the fact that the gas in the Photon Bus' tank was half the price of the 2008 peak. Nor was I thinking about the fact that the race for more expensively-produced shale oil in the U.S. and Canada was ignited by OPEC slowing their own production, creating a nine-year run of high barrel prices. With increased domestic production in North America, OPEC finds it no longer holds all the cards. Well, OPEC never liked playing Texas Hold Em.

We pulled up to the junction with Highway 46 at Blackwell's Corner. At the corner gas station we saw a huge image of James Dean's head emerging from a garland of orange flowers. This was to commemorate that this station was the last place James Dean filled his Porsche 550 Spyder before getting killed in a head-on collision with a Ford Tudor Coupe twenty-six miles up the road. It was an inviting memorial. It made the Texaco station seem more historic than other gas stations. I chose not to fill up with historically priced gas.

Barb doesn't know it yet, but I plan to put in my will that I would like a large image of me placed at the last gas station I fill up. People will say, "Hey, there's that station where old Bill filled up." Maybe, if all gas stations sported memorial images, we would feel better paying whatever price the industry has decided to charge us.

I let Siri guide us through Paso Robles into Morro Bay. It seems the ghost of Edsgar Dijkstra needed one more laugh. The lurid voice of Siri instructed us to drive through rolling, picturesque wine country, a balm after witnessing the terra firma abattoir of the oil fields. Suddenly, she demanded a left turn into a quaint country road. It had a quaint name, Old Creek Road.

After a few innocent miles, Old Creek Road became an old, narrow-laned, no-shoulder, twisted nightmare. A tunnel of cowering oak trees missed us by inches. To avoid the trees, I had to edge into the opposite lane. Hanging branches crashed into the windshield. Barb developed a sudden case of the "slow downs." I winced at every turn with apprehension an oncoming vehicle would appear. There was not enough room on the road. Siri!

One time I got mad at Siri and called her an idiot. She replied, "Oh, I'm blushing." Now she was wreaking her non-blushing revenge. I'm sure she colluded with Shakey the Robot.

After eight psychiatric miles we made it to the Pacific Coast Highway. The ocean looked like an inviting afterlife. We glided into the Morrow Dunes RV Park. The office was spacious and several employees were at their desks typing or talking on the phone. I felt like I was reporting for duty. I asked them if there was a better way to get to Morro Bay than Old Creek Road. They looked shocked. "You didn't go that way did you? Why would you go that way?" I explained I was at the mercy of my GPS since I was unfamiliar with the area. A woman said, with force, "Somebody should call them!"

We backed into a circular area that held five camping spots. I could see the ocean out the kitchen window. The sound of waves and the familiar aroma of salt water floated in from the beach. This would be the best RV park of the trip and Morro Bay would yield some of the best images. A storm was coming, but we were tucked in.

Pumpjacks sucking black gold

Chapter 17

To Morro Bay Today

Blessed and burdened with two defining landmarks, Morro Bay is named after a rock. Hopefully, it will fare better than Rhyolite. The word morro in Spanish, or Italian, means prominent rock. Morro Rock is a 576-foot high volcanic plug that lords over the entrance to Morro Bay. Like Portland's Mount Hood, it is visible all over town.

The other structures visible all over town, and towering over the Embarcadero tourist strip, are the three 450-foot stacks of the Morro Bay Power Plant. Town folk have hominified the stacks as The Three Fingers. There was only one stack after construction in 1955. One wonders what the original nickname was.

The storm rolled over our cozy camp with stinging, salty gusts wailing against the sidewalls of the Photon Bus. I walked to the beach, curious. A mare's tail of white whistled off the top of Morro Rock, streaming like a scream over the stacks, whose red top-lights looked like candy cigarettes. Moonlight shimmered in glowing ghost canyons in the clouds. A windsock vibrated like a snare drum. The image of the mare's tail and the luminous stacks hit me, like Ansel Adams at Hernandez. It was a shot. It was chilly. I brought out the gear and shot long exposures, stabilizing the tripod in the sand with both hands.

The next morning, during my photography ritual, I loaded the images into Lightroom and started throwing sliders. The images looked black. Had I underexposed everything, another rookie mistake? A push on the exposure slider unveiled some nice images. As I fine tuned the many parameters of the Develop Module, I felt the wave of pleasure that photographers and artists experience when bathing in the delight of creation.

Long-exposures look different from the scene the eye remembers. The camera's sensor harvests photons over a much longer interval than the recharge rate of the eye's rods and cones. Areas that were dim, or shadow, now pop out with much greater luminance on the captured image. During development, you see an image born that is excitingly brighter, more dramatic, than what resonates in the mind.

I was so excited I emailed the pictures to the Morro Dunes RV Park and wrote that they had my permission to use the images on their website. I showed the pictures on my phone to one of the office women, who said, "Yes, those are nice," with muted enthusiasm. I suppose they have seen lots of photos of their town from hopped up tourists.

Morro Bay, day two, the rain let up, but a new front massed over the Pacific that wasn't. I reserved another night in our asphalt harbor. We set out to explore Morro Bay with rain gear in our packs and the joy of exploration in our hearts. The beach trail led over the new bridge at Morro Creek, past the power plant.

Dynegy now owns the plant, which previously employed over a hundred workers. It is probably permanently closed as it would require expensive upgrades to meet current air quality standards. There is talk of putting in a tidal power station that could use the plant's transmission infrastructure.

Strolling down the Embarcadero, Morro Bay struck me as an idealized version of a beach town. This was not the San Francisco Embarcadero with ocean liner moorage and a brooding, concrete-and-glass financial district. This was a fishing village with inviting restaurants and shops festooned with all the stuff we tourists expect to see any time we're in sight of the ocean. Gulls perched on car roofs. Bright orange aloe plants demanded face time everywhere. The sidewalk sculpture of a worn-out Ford truck bench seat was almost too realistic. It was deeply relaxing, a good place to wander aimlessly, a Zen non-destiny.

We found one of the main attractions, the raft of resident sea otters at the T-pier. The sea otters are local celebrities. Adults float on their backs, babies resting on mother's bellies. Fur traders hunted these Disney ready mammals to near extinction until the Fur Seal Treaty of 1911 ended the slaughter. Mostly it was Russians taking furs, but Putin now states that Russia had nothing to do with the American sea otter problem.

The otters were believed extinct until locals discovered a lone raft off Big Sur in 1938. The population has recovered and numbers are spiking due to tasty urchins, exploding like tidal weeds because of a massive die-off of sea stars from a wasting disease. The slow one now will later be fast, or at least well fed.

For the last week, Barb had sought, like Joan of Arc, to find a Post Office. The Post Office played hide and seek, giggling at Barb's growing stack of letters. After breakfast in a diner, we headed uphill through neighborhoods to where a tourist map said there was an Office. After the great relief of getting letters into the mail, we hiked toward Black Hill, a local summit that overlooked the Bay.

Hard rain obscured the view of the bay, so we headed back to Morro Rock. En route a friendly local who ran a tree service informed us the interesting conifer we had seen was a Norfolk Pine. At Morro Rock, we made friends with a juvenile Western Sea Gull. His parents placed a rainbow across the bay just for us. It was one of those days where you sense years of stress evaporate off your skin.

It stormed most of the night, but the next morning the radar looked good heading north. We headed out for Monterey

Bay, hoping for another landing as sweet as Morro Bay.

Ghost Canyons

Mare's tail off Morro Rock

Bridge over Morro Creek

Gift from a seagull

Chapter 18

Half Moon Bay, Full Wind Night

Again, the nightly storm that had tracked us since Santa Fe, died down by morning. We prepared for a run through the weather gauntlet to Monterey Bay. I booked a night at Moss Landing.

We avoided the horror of Old Creek Road and drove up Highway 1 to Highway 46 and over to Route 101, over the Coast Range, almost too verdant with hills that looked like waves of green felt. We continued north on 101 into the Salinas Valley, Steinbeck country. The Salinas River, named because it becomes salty from upwelling tides, ran northwest and emptied into Monterey Bay.

Most major highways follow paths worked out centuries, or millennia, ago by migrating herds, Paleo-Indians or early explorers. U.S. Route 101 follows the 1775 trail of Juan Bautista de Anza, a captain of New Spain, which desired to colonize Alta California to oppose Russian ingression. Perhaps they feared for the sea otters?

Another explorer, Juan Rodriguez Cabrillo, namesake of Pacific Coast Highway 1, was not impressed by the state that would later honor him. Natives along the coast were hunter-gatherers living in scattered, small bands with no agriculture and, Oye Dios, no gold. They were nothing like the Aztecs or the Mayas.

Perhaps the name, California, had been optimistic given Cabrillo's report. California is the name of an island of beautiful single-breasted Amazon warriors in Greek mythology. The conquistadors could not have foreseen that two centuries later a movie about an Amazon superhero, Wonder Woman, 93% on Rotten Tomatoes, would be made in the real California and would play at El Con, a mall in Tucson named after conquistodors!

Gaspar de Portolà founded the first two colonies in Alta California at San Diego and Monterey in 1769. Volunteers for colonization were hard to find since the route north from New Spain was brutal. By sea ships had to battle southerly prevailing winds and the California current. Travel through the waterless land route up the Baja Peninsula, also no fun.

de Anza looked for a more accommodating passage. He started at the Tubac Presidio, now home of the Tin Cup golf course and over-priced Mexican food, and crossed the Colorado River at Yuma. This route became the Camino Real, now Highway 101.

New Spain established twenty one missions along the California coast. First, New Spain kicked out the Jesuits because they feared the power of the Jesuit Order. Then, newly independent Mexico secularized all the missions to extinguish the power of the Catholic Church. There was much fear of power. There still is.

All the right people, well-connected colonists, received mission lands after independence, deeded as Ranchos. The padres, as padres tend to do, treated the Indians as Catholic-converted slaves. Even after the missions closed, the Indians, still enslaved at the bottom of the power curve, received mandatory jobs as Rancho-hands.

We traveled, de Anza-like, through prime Rancho country, not all of which has been developed into prime suburban real estate. The Salinas Valley, called America's Salad Bowl, is still agricultural and is productive. North of Soledad we drove by the largest vineyard I've ever seen, the rows spreading as far as the eye could see. Now we can enjoy a nice Cabernet with our salad.

Moss Landing was another parking-lot style RV camp, but clean with nice bathrooms. It rained buckets that night, but cleared by morning. We walked over the harbor bridge to the Old Salinas River and explored Salinas State Beach. I saw no surfers on the storm-steroided waves.

We played storm leap-frog the next day and drove up to Half Moon Bay, where we found a high-priced, no-bathroom, concrete park with a stunning view of the bay. I washed the Bus in our camping site before Barb told me about the sign. A neighbor camper pulled out fishing rods, brand new gear. I asked about the fishing. He didn't know. He invited me to go with him and his son.

We tried fishing in the vicious surf on the other side of the marina. None of us had waders. We ran madly through the surf as the angry sea chased us. It was a Hemingway of a sea. We gave up fishing and caught lunch at a Taco Bell right on the beach, the highest grossing Taco Bell in the nation according to my new friend. My fishing buddy, recently divorced, bought a trailer to live in full-time and was recreating through his bucket list at hyper speed: fishing, kite-surfing lessons, sky-diving. There's worse ways to rebound.

The winds picked up as evening approached. Through the windshield in the comfort of our motorized beach house we watched kite-surfers in the marina and a pair of fearless traditional surfers getting ripping waves off the jetty.

Then Poseidon showed up. I had experienced Poseidon years ago when we were on the Greek Island of Samos in the Icarian Sea. A storm came in from the Mediterranean at night. Sheet lightning in the sky made flashing bowls of light in the clouds that repeated every few seconds. P-man raved for hours.

He destroyed the dock at Pythagoreio. Remember the Pythagorean theorem? There were no more right angles, no hypotenuses, at that dock.

This night, Poseidon unleashed from his trident a furious wind that shook the Photon Bus. Barb thought we would tip over. We put the slides in, but the rock-and-roll concert continued. Staring at a swaying reading light in our land yacht, I flashed on the fact that my jacks, one-inch diameter steel posts, supported the entire weight of the Bus. I imagined the jacks bending like taffy and took them in.

What good is a storm if you don't walk out into it? I could barely force the door against thirty mph winds. Poseidon didn't go home to Amphitrite until the wee hours. She was pissed. She threw his trident in the garbage after his all night storming. I wish I could have sent Shakey the Robot after him.

A dilapidated, old Winnebago sat rusting in the slot next to us. It had a trailer court, shanty ambience. When I emerged from our haven that morning, the occupant of the shanty was working on his engine. He had overalls and looked like a grown-up farm boy. We chatted. He was an electrical engineer who had come out from Ohio to work on the spaceship.

The spaceship? It was the new headquarters of Apple, Apple Park, a one-mile circular, 2.8 million square-foot campus in Cupertino. He had driven from Ohio and needed a place to stay so he bought the old Winnebago and rented a scenic spot overlooking the bay, better than an apartment. The Winnebago was pretty much down to scrap metal. When his job finished, he planned to buy a new truck and a new trailer to haul back to Ohio. He knew Barb's home town, Napoleon. They chatted in the friendly manner of Midwesterners.

Apple Park is the last vision of Steve Jobs who also designed the Pixar campus. Jobs hired architect Norman Foster and told him to think about a marriage of London Square and the Main Quad of Stanford University. Apple secretly accumulated one hundred seventy-five acres then sprung the plan on the Cupertino City Council, which made a show of debating for six hours before unanimously approving the project. Duh!

The inner, open-air sanctum of the circle has fruit trees, apples for Apple. For unveilings of new products, a performance that Jobs turned into an art form, the Steve Jobs Theater can house a thousand blissful acolytes. The building will run on one hundred percent renewable energy from solar and biofuel. For nine months of the year it will need neither air conditioning nor heating thanks to a natural ventilation system. It will recycle 157,000 gallons of water a day. There are 11,000 underground parking spaces with 700 electric charging stations. I wonder if Apple needs any recycled surgeons?

The sun came out and wanted to play. We walked up the beach to Sam's Chowder House and had a seafood lunch on the patio overlooking the bay. I classify any restaurant meal as overpriced, but after a night of Poseidon playing the Aeolian P-funk the view of the shining bay and blue sky brought tranquility. In a way, we were enjoying the last meal of the trip, since we would drive back to Stockton to my brother's house, back in familiar territory, no longer exploring the never seen.

Verdant hills of the Coastal Range

Last supper at Sam's Chowderhouse

Chapter 19

Requiem for a Voyage

We lumbered out of Half Moon Bay, chugged over a gnarly pass, barreled across the San Mateo Bridge and trundled into the freeway web of the East Bay. With Siri instructing on probation, we took I-580 to I-5 to Stockton. We exited at the familiar ramp to my brother's house, West Benjamin Holt Drive.

In 1883, Benjamin Holt and his brothers moved their wagon wheel company to Stockton so they could season the wooden wheels against dry rot in the warm climate of the Central Valley. Holt, an ace mechanic, made his first steam tractor in 1890, Old Betsy, a single-piston, sixty-horsepower behemoth that carried six hundred seventy-five gallons of fuel and weighed 48,000 pounds, almost three times the weight of the Photon Bus with one-sixth the horsepower.

The Holt Manufacturing Company built the first successful track-driven tractor in 1904. Holt Caterpillars hauled artillery guns to the battlefields of World War I. The British and French noticed these Yank Tanks and got the idea to build military tanks on tracks that could crawl over trenches. Only slightly indirectly, Benjamin Holt helped bring about an end to the "war to end all wars," which unfortunately did not end all wars, which seem to have no end.

Tree branches littered every street in Stockton. I needed a Holt track-drive driving down his Drive. The scene was wet and dreary. We holed up at John's for two days waiting for the front to clear in the north. There was no golf to be had.

We visited John's sloop at the Stockton Yacht Club. The Club, decorated with nautical trappings, had a jaunty maritime feel. But John had lost his enthusiasm for sailing on the San Joaquin River and the byzantine canals of the Delta. Also, he was tired of the moorage fees. His boat partner planned to sail the old sloop through the Delta to Napa and find a new moorage. Aloha boat.

The radar looked clear. We bolted up Benjamin Holt Drive and took a drive up I-5. At Shasta Pass, three foot snow banks lined the interstate, but the tarmac was dry. When we crossed the Oregon border it rained and didn't stop for four months.

Our house looked like a war zone. Downed branches and leaves covered every inch of lawn. A Sword of Damocles hung over the Bus' parking spot. It took two days to clean and repair party damage in the house. The arborists came and left a large pile of bark dust for the garden.

Then, I didn't know what to do. Engaged in the daily diversions of the road, I had not faced retirement life. After many years of heavy responsibility to patients and round-the-clock availability, I had no desire to seek volunteer work. I've worked!

My years as a surgeon were shrouded with an ever-present chance of needing to drop whatever I was doing and tend to someone's emergency. When I was younger and full of energy, it was exciting. All surgeons live with a constant underground rumble of anxiety, the specter of complications, the patient that suddenly goes bad.

All that looming stress was technically gone, but the creature with red eyes still crept around in my attic, waiting for me to dream. My reflexes were too ingrained. I kept reaching to my belt on the right side, checking for the pager that was no longer there. Traveling had kept my mind occupied for the first two months of retirement. Now I was home, not traveling.

I worked up songs on guitar. I learned the leads to Comfortably Numb and Hotel California on my Martin. Then I got an idea. Maybe I should write a book?

CHAPTER 20

THE RV INDUSTRY IS BOOMING

The Recreational Vehicle Industry is booming with optimism. Total RV shipments in January of 2017, as reported on the Recreational Vehicle Industry Association, RVIA, website, are 33,859, up 7.4% from one year ago. Most sales, 28,931, are towable trailers. Motorhome shipments for January are up 15.2% at 4,928 units. Total RV shipments in 2016 (430,961) were the highest in 40 years of record. Yes, there is optimism in the $15 billion-per-year Industry.

Historical data back to 1978 shows wild swings in total yearly RV shipments, from a high of 390,500 in 2006 to a low of 107,200 in 1980. Curiously, 1978, two years before the 1980 nadir, was a banner year at 389,900 shipments.

One would expect the number of RV shipments, driven by preceding total purchases, to vary with economic indicators. Recreational Vehicles, since they are for recreation, are purchased with disposable income, although a small percentage of owners live in their RV full time. Perhaps it should be no surprise that the graph of RV Shipments mirrors the DOW Jones Industrial Average.

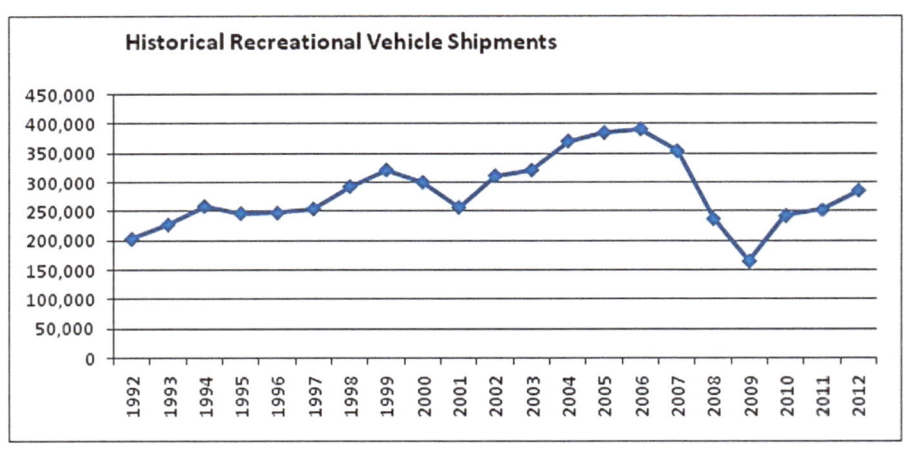

RV Shipments, 1992-2012

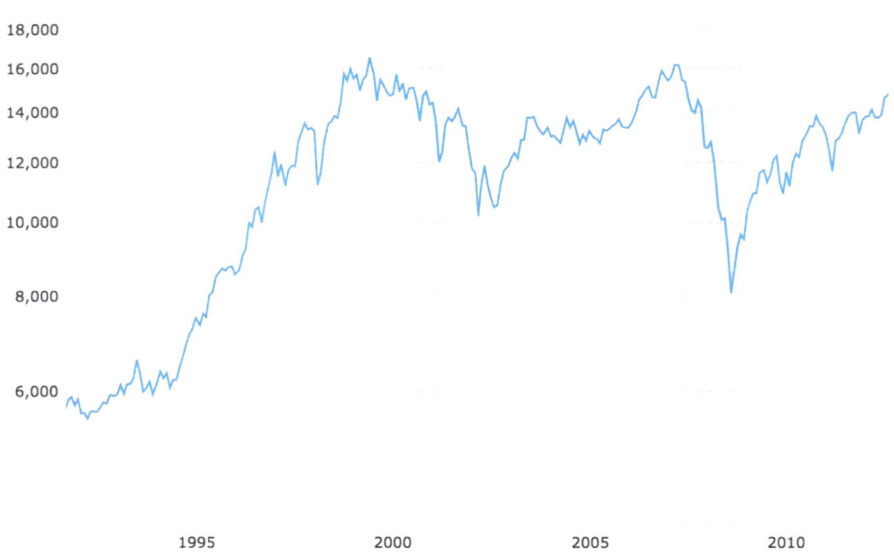

Dow Jones Industrial Average, 1992-2012

The Baby Boom generation, those born 1946 to 1964, my generation (talkin' bout my generation: The Who), is already marching through the gates of retirement, which we all hope is long before the other gate we will go through. Industries gearing up for the Boomer retirement, range from healthcare (implants, organs, erections, etc.) to the pet industry to wine growers to prostate diapers.

There may be a dark side to the swelling tsunami of retirement, an elderly bust to the Baby Boom. Not all Boomers have adequate savings for retirement. A GoBankingRates survey found thirty percent of those over age fifty-five had no, read zero, retirement savings and an additional twenty-six percent had less than fifty thousand saved. A large percentage, possibly the majority, of Boomer retirees will not have sufficient income from Social Security to live a modest, secure lifestyle. The dependency ratio is the ratio of those outside working age to those inside working age (18-64). This ratio was fifty-nine in 2010, but will rise to seventy-five by 2030. There will be fewer and fewer working age citizens supporting more and more retired elderly.

So, not every Boomer will have the dough to buy an RV, at least for recreational purposes. But there is still reason for optimism in the Industry. The demographic with the largest growth in RV ownership is the Millennial generation, age 35 to 54. Maybe these young RV owners will take heart and give a ride to Baby Boomers shuffling between work camps.

The RV Industry is not only the manufacturing sector; it encompasses dealerships and sales, RV parks and resorts, service-related businesses such as mechanical and repair services, retail stores like Camping World and Walmart, trade shows, conventions and a large number of trade and consumer organizations and websites.

According to RVIA-commissioned research, the Industry

had a $50 billion economic impact in 2015, including $7.9 billion in wages for 150,000 jobs. The RV Industry accounted for two percent of the total U.S. GDP in 2015, whereas, the gluttonous Healthcare Industry consumed almost eighteen percent of GDP, totaling $3.2 trillion.

I don't know, I think I'd rather explore beautiful places and drive back roads than have a knee replacement, that is, if I could afford either one.

Chapter 21

RV Construction for Idiots

When I purchased my RVs, I knew next to nothing about their construction. I didn't know the type or make of the chassis, the construction technique (frame rail or semi-monocoque), the side wall materials, the roof materials, the type of windows, the cabinetry quality, the plumbing materials or anything I could not directly see when viewing the vehicle on the lot. Who would purchase a high-price, complex system that your life depends on without knowing everything possible about its construction?

You, in the back, raise your hand. The answer is: most of us. Most of us make car purchasing decisions based on visual appeal, manufacturer reputation, friend's comments or subliminal messages we got from TV ads while watching Seinfeld re-runs. I did little research on RV construction until I wrote this book. That's wrong. I did zero research on RV construction. My advice is, if you want to buy an RV, write a book first.

Chassis are important. Chassis are like the foundation of our homes; we don't see them or know they are there unless something goes wrong like a flood or a hurricane or an earthquake. Randall Eaton's *Motorhome Comparison Guide* has an excellent chapter called, "What to look for in a motorhome chassis". He explains terms like "wheel cut" and "wheelbase" and discusses the difference between a single rear axle versus a double rear axle, also known as a tagged axle. Tagged axles reduce the wandering sensation when driving. I would like to try one someday.

Semi-monocoque construction, found in high-end motorhomes, adds cross-bracing to the basic factory frame, which increases frame strength and decreases the amount of twisting the frame will undergo during stress. A true monocoque construction means the skin of the vehicle is a load-bearing structural element. Monocoque, from the French, means single shell. The ultimate monocoque construction is a bird egg. Less expensive than semi-monocoque, body-on-frame construction assembles the floor and walls on an unmodified chassis. The Coachman website states: "Gas Class A Motorhomes are built on a rail motor vehicle chassis powered by a front gas engine." So, my Pursuit 31SB does not have a semi-monocoque construction.

The Coachman Pursuit has a Ford F-53 Super Duty Motorhome Chassis, Gross Vehicle Weight Rating (GVWR) 18,000 pounds. The wheelbase is 208 inches. A longer wheelbase can support more weight, more GVWR. The rear frame width is 34 inches, which became important knowledge when I upgraded the receiver hitch.

Ready-to-go chassis, like the F-53, come with an engine, brakes, steering system, drivetrain, transmission, wheels, tires, axles, shock absorbers, cooling and heating systems, battery and electrical system, fuel tank and exhaust system. You could attach a driver's seat and drive your chassis down the road. Someone should do that. It would look cool and maybe make the national TV news.

Many manufacturers use ready-to-go chassis, although some do custom modifications on their own. Eighty percent of Gas Class A Motorhomes are built on Ford Chassis, with most of the rest on Chevrolet Chassis. The Workhorse W-series Chassis coupled with an 8.1 L GM Vortec V8 engine was popular, but Navistar, who bought the company in 2005, discontinued production in 2012. Workhorse Chassis owners can still bond by joining *The Workhorse Chassis Motorhome Club*.

Owners of all the major chassis brands can discuss issues on .iRV2 Forums in one of the six Chassis Club forums. The Ford Chassis forum has 3,934 threads on 79 pages, but the Workhorse forum has 7,617 threads on 101 pages. What does this mean? Do Workhorse Chassis have more problems than Ford or are Workhorse Chassis owners more passionate and, therefore, more likely to go on forums? The great utility of the various forums is that you can find a thread about any problem you encounter. Detailed posts come from owners who have deep mechanical knowledge of the product.

As Jerry Seinfeld might ask, "What's the big deal about a chassis?" Well, the obvious functions of a chassis are to hold the engine and wheels and other important components of the drive system. In motorhomes, the chassis is asked to support, and be the foundation of, the considerable weight of a mini-home that will be driven over vibration-inducing road surfaces. Yikes!

The chassis transmits road vibrations, a major factor in the smoothness of the ride. So, Jerry, the chassis influences many of the drivability features sought by RV owners and the people who are sometimes forced to ride in RVs on long, boring road trips with their parents, who are boring and so are their friends and how much farther is it?

Chassis are a major factor in determining the interior sound level. All first-time RV owners learn the same thing on the ride home from the dealer. RVs are noisy. Compared to cars, RVs are really noisy. A good chassis that absorbs road vibrations and has solid connections between cabinetry and floor can minimize squeaks and rattles.

Owners must take some of the blame for noise. How one packs items makes a big difference. Are towels around your pots and pans? Is your silverware loose or in a tight-fitting drawer liner? Could someone go right now and take those damn reading glasses off the hook above the couch???

The biggest, heaviest and most expensive chassis are on

the macho diesel pushers. Diesel pushers are the beefy kings of the RV motorhome world. The major Class A Diesel chassis manufacturers are Freightliner, Spartan and Roadmaster. A few manufacturers build chassis from scratch, but most modify a factory model.

Each chassis manufacturer will tout unique modifications or components that make theirs the smoothest ride and the safest foundation for your home-in-the-wind. I had never heard of "torque induced drive line grumble," but the Spartan K3 chassis, 24,000 lb. GVWR, reduces that. I'm all for reducing the amount of grumbling, because we planned this trip carefully and we will not go home early and when you are older you will spend all your spring breaks with your friends, so can't you enjoy these last few years with your parents?

Manufacturers that do their own modifications to a stripped chassis give the chassis a proprietary name. Tiffen, a family owned company in Red Bay, Alabama, offers the Powerglide Chassis for their Allegro models. Instead of welds, the Powerglide is assembled with non-removable Huck Bolts, tightened to 27,000 lbs. torque. Heck! To reduce rattle, The Powerglide has anti-camber rails on subfloors, Tuthill independent front suspension and Bilstein shocks. A unique Vansco Multiplex electrical system routes all electrics into a computerized bus. It comes with the popular Cummins Diesel 600-hp engine and Allison transmission.

Winnebago has the Evolution with increased center section clearance due to precision rail placement. It also has the Maxum with a 55 degree wheel cut. These are names that sound more like sports cars than mere chassis. Freightliner makes the Liberty Chassis, which has a V-ride suspension to give better roll stability. Newmar modifies chassis with their own welded foundation, dubbed the STAR Chassis. Ford, ever sober, makes several motorhome chassis, including my F53. At least they add the term Super Duty, so us Ford drivers can have a little pride. My vehicle is capable of more than regular duty.

Chassis are sturdy monuments of steel and fire and are likely to outlast all the other structures and systems of our RVs. One forum commenter wondered if he had a "35-year chassis." A respondent stated, "What does it matter? Everything else will break before that. None of us are going to be driving our motorhomes for 35 years anyway." It reminds me of the discussion one night at Portland Photographic about which was the ideal file type for RAW files that would be compatible with future software. A senior member commented, "What does it matter? No one will look at our pictures after we're dead." Ah, mortality.

After chassis construction, the next step is building floors, walls and roofs on the platform. Older models used "stick and tin" construction with wood frames covered by aluminum or fiberglass. Wood has a nice strength-to-weight ratio and has sound-dampening capability. But, wood has a major drawback. Water will work its way through even the best constructed exterior and cause mold and rot and cause delamination of laminated exterior skins. This is more of a factor now with the omnipresent slideouts. Aluminum or steel frames will not rot.

The salesman proudly pointed out the exterior skin on my Pursuit is a new blended polypropylene and fiberglass composite known as Azdel. As explained by Steve, on You Tube, Azdel is light, fifty percent lighter than wood, but is strong and puncture resistant. In the video Steve brings out two water-filled mason jars, one with the Azdel sidewall and another with a luan-laminated fiberglass, that had been soaking for three years. Three years! The water in the laminate jar was brown and, according to Steve, had a foul odor. The Azdel jar was crystal clear. Heck, you could drink it. I feel good about Azdel. Delamination fear is a thing of the past. One tip, don't use Liquid Wrench to clean bird droppings off your Azdel sidewall.

We all like a good roof. Good roofs are the vanguard of civilization. So what's the best roof for a motorhome? As I have learned, one visit to an Open Roads Forum was worth several hours of Google searching. The high-end manufacturers make molded fiberglass roofs and point out that fiberglass will not tear like a rubber roof or deform like an aluminum roof. From the Forum: "If your roof is hit by the toilet seat from the Russian Mir, it won't ever get scratched." Rubber roofs are either EPDM, Ethylene Propylene Diene Monomer, or TPO, Thermal Poly Olefin. Which of these are better? Hang on.

Here's a summary of comments from the forum. I think these comments from actual users of the materials are far more valuable than the industry trade pitches.

All roofs work and all need maintenance. Leaks come from the holes made for vent pipes, antennas, air conditioners, etc.

Owner of an aluminum roof: "Over time it developed pinholes all over the roof…"

Owner of a fiberglass roof: "I have molded fiberglass and it's no end of problems."

Owner of an aluminum roof: "I thought an aluminum roof was best until I camped under tall chestnut trees. My roof now resembles a golf ball with dimples all over it."

Owner of an EDPM rubber roof: "Our 5er is now 13 years old. I check our roof twice a year. We have never had a roof leak so far…"

Comment about TPO rubber: "Seems that if moisture gets under them, the felt backing will wick to large areas…EPDM…doesn't seem to wick."

I feel OK about the EPDM rubber roof on my Pursuit. The rain is fairly loud, but would be even louder with either fiberglass or aluminum.

I've learned something about RV construction. Would this knowledge have changed my decision to purchase the Pursuit? Probably not. I still like having that big screen TV right across from the couch.

Chapter 22

How Not To Purchase An RV

    I am a discriminating consumer. I research purchases on Google and on Amazon and read lots of consumer reviews, both the four-star and the one- and two-star. For example, I bought a motor scooter to carry on the back of my RV. To educate my decision, I looked at details like weight, horsepower, tire size, luggage capacity and mileage. Then I test rode the top two candidates. I liked the Yamaha Smax, more powerful than the Honda, with a top speed of 80 mph. It is freeway legal and gets 85 miles per gallon.

    Once I knew what I wanted, I searched for the best price and found a good deal on a new 2015 model, no different than the 2017, at a surprisingly large dealership in the small town of Sublimity, forty miles from my house. Although I haven't ridden the Smax much, I feel confident I have made a good choice.

    So why did I abandon my usual caution when I bought both my RVs? When I researched for my first RV, I looked only at prices. I knew little about construction or manufacturers. With scant knowledge in the old noodle, I drove to a dealership and inspected models on the lot. I found a used Catalina, but didn't immediately purchase it.

    Barb is more frugal than I am and I'm pretty frugal. She grew up in a working class family and has a reflexive resistance to purchasing anything. I knew she would resist my proposal to buy the Class C Catalina.

She did. "We don't need that." I unrolled my arguments a little at a time. This would be good for the family. Our son, Joshua, who did not like tent camping, would agree to travel with us. RV trips were cheaper than flying and renting a car. I think her memories of camping in a tent trailer with her family kicked in and she agreed to look at the RV. When we walked up the retractable steps into the living space of the Catalina, she said something that signaled we would be taking it home. She said the same thing that every buyer on the show, *Going RV*, says when they like an interior or a feature. Oh wow! You can predict which RV they will choose by the Oh-Wow count.

So what information did I process to choose this motorhome? Did I inquire about the engine specs, the chassis, the sidewall construction (aluminum, steel or wood), the sidewall skin material (aluminum or fiberglass), the windows (single or double pane), the flooring, the insulation material, the roof material (vinyl, rubber or fiberglass), slideouts (number and type, electric or hydraulic), the transmission, the torque converter, the electronics, the air conditioner brand and BTU output, the generator brand and capacity, the holding tank size, the plumbing (copper or PEX pipe), the jacks (manual or automatic), the awning (manual or electric), the cabinet construction (particle board or solid wood), the age of the used tires, the gas mileage, the maintenance history, the tow capacity, the manufacturer reputation and rating, the dealer reputation or the likelihood that the cosmic background radiation represents the border of our universe?

No! I hear my father in my brain. Don't be a meat-head! I didn't inquire about any of these important qualitative facts. I was like most first-time buyers when they walk into an RV on a lot or at a trade show. They picture themselves and their family lounging in the living area with a beautiful outdoor scene glowing outside the windows.

A 2011 report by Richard T. Curtin at the University of

Michigan Survey Research Center, cited price as the most common reason for selecting a particular RV (39%), followed by interior space (35%), the number of sleeping spaces (31%) and workmanship-and-styling (29%).

When I bought my motorhome I based my decision on my initial impression of the interior. The Catalina had walnut veneer cabinets with glass inlay that was ranch-house chic. The upholstery, a natural muted color with a coarse weave, looked tough. Kids would love the bunk bed over the cab. A little voice said this would be comfortable quarters for camping and traveling. Don't worry if you track in a little mud.

Over eight years of enjoying our family RV, I learned a lot about the use of an RV and developed preferences of what I wanted in an upgrade. I researched, in my wishbooking manner, hundreds of Class As and fine-tuned my preferences, focusing on three items: a booth diner that faced a couch, a large screen TV at eye level and a decor that was not ostentatious.

If I didn't see these qualities when viewing the images on RV Trader, I moved on. Decors in the high-end Class A models turned me off. The popular oval recessed ceiling mirrors with surrounding LED lights was more bordello than camping. The fancy backsplashes and engraved, dark hardwood cabinets put me in the mind of the many urban mega-hotels I had stayed in for surgery meetings. I wanted to feel like I was camping in the outdoors instead of schmoozing in a politically charged lobby.

My grade should be an F minus for not following the advice of websites and books that instruct potential RV buyers what to look for and what to inspect when buying a used or new RV. I have now done the good research I should have done before. But I have found no teacher who would allow me to turn my work in late. Hence, I still have the F minus. But I also have my new Class A Coachman Pursuit. I have an F and an A. What can I expect?

One aspect I failed to research was the reputation of the

manufacturer, Coachman. I saw a lot of Coachmans on the road, so I formed a vague sense they must be good quality because, hey, a lot of people drive them. When I was growing up, Volkswagen Beetles were ubiquitous, and I formed the notion they were reliable and desirable automobiles.

After college, I bought a used Volkswagen 1302 S Super Beetle, which had a more powerful engine (60-hp, 1600cc) than the basic Beetle. The neighbor I bought it from showed me how to adjust the valve clearance, which I did every 6 months as long as I owned it.

The Super Beetle was a great car. I drove it several times from Tucson to Atlanta where I attended Emory University Medical School. I drove it to Maine and to Key West and when I interviewed for surgery residencies, I drove it all over the American West. I visited every extreme corner of America including Presque Isle, Maine; Key West, Florida; Seattle, Washington; and San Diego, California. It ran like a top. I slept in a tent or crunched in the back seat on my marathon drives.

The alternator went out in San Francisco. I was staying at my friend's parent's friend's house in Palo Alto. The wife helped me go to a junkyard, find a used alternator and replace it. She handed me tools and seemed excited about the project. I got the impression that mechanics was an interesting change of pace for her.

I traded the Super Beetle for a Toyota FJ40, the original box-shaped FJ. I was crushed to say goodbye to my valiant blue steed, who had served me well over so much time and distance. The paltry trade-in price offended me and I recited to the salesman an emotionally charged description of my travels in my blue friend. The description of high mileage road travel was likely not a good selling point, but the salesman was sympathetic. He wanted to make a sale.

Most of us develop distinct tastes about our automobiles. Most of sleep fairly close to our metal warrior steeds. Our urban-sprawled cities are designed around the automobile.

New York is the only urban center where more commuters use public transportation than cars. Fifty-four percent of New Yorkers use public transit, whereas in Portland, a city awarded for urban planning and admired for its light rail, only thirteen percent ride the rails or buses. As you go east to west in America, the percentage of commuters using public transit plummets. We westerners liked our horses. Now we like our cars and trucks.

So how bad or good were my uninformed and poorly researched RV purchases?

The Catalina took us on some great trips over an eight year period. When I purchased it, it was six years old with 12,000 miles. When I sold it, it was fourteen years old with 40,000 miles. There were repairs. The Onan generator quit working the first winter. The Cummins shop on Swan Island replaced the carburetor which fixed the problem. The mechanic explained what many RV owners know: gasoline, when left standing for months at a time, will precipitate a varnish that can clog lines. He recommended using a gas stabilizing additive.

The Catalina wouldn't start right before the Crater Lake trip. I had it towed to my mechanic where I was embarrassed to learn the battery cables were loose. The biggest expense was the transmission. On its last recreational trip the Catalina required a lot of revving to overcome inertia. It conked out at a traffic light. My worthy mechanic, Tom, discovered a leak in the transmission cooling line. The cooling line was metal and so was the bracket attaching it to the metal chassis. There was no buffer inside the bracket, so it had worn a hole and spilled four gallons of transmission fluid. Over a few hundred miles the torque converter over revved, generating enough heat to cook the clutch plates.

There were other problems. There was delamination on the right front sidewall and possibly a water leak at the roof joint. I had to rebuild one of the cabinet drawers, held together by staples. I tired of the carbon monoxide alarm going off and replaced it with a battery powered unit. The microwave died just before I traded it in. Other than the transmission burn-out, most of the systems held up over 28,000 miles of travel. Impressive. How long would any of our home appliances hold up over thousands of miles of the constant vibration of road travel?

Now I have another Coachman. After I bought the Catalina, several people told me they thought Coachman was a good brand. After purchasing my second Coachman, I wondered, at long last, how Coachman stacked up against the other brands. Meat-head!

You can find answers to almost any question about RVs on several web discussion forums like RV Forum Community. Forums are godsends in solving problems. Forum posts discuss the ins and outs of RV life in great detail. The tone of discourse is refreshingly mature, the opposite of the adolescent trolls one finds on, say, YouTube.

The topic, Coachman Quality?, on RV Forum has been visited 12,252 times. The Coachman gets mixed reviews. A common comment is "entry level."

So what do the people say?

From a Forum Staff:

Personally I would not buy any Coachman product. It is low entry level quality, even in the models that are trimmed up to look like higher priced rigs. And I find their designs quirky, even more so than even the typical RV foibles. Coachman products sell well in areas where the RV season is short and usage limited - the low price makes the limited usage more palatable, and with low use the lower quality materials and workmanship are less of an issue.

From G———-:

I personally do not have any experience with Coachman, but there is a guy out in front of the local Camping World/American RV dealership with a homemade sign that reads, "DO NOT BUY A COACHMAN". Maybe you could ask him. (This may be the dealership I purchased from!)

From a Forum Staff who actually owned a Coachman:

We did own a Coachman. In 1989 we bought a used 1986 Class C. Put over 100,000 miles on it in 14 years. Never had a single problem related to the Coachman brand. Did have refrigerator and furnace problems. Yes, it's a low entry level coach but that's all some people need or can afford for occasional weekend/vacation use.

Forest River purchased Coachman in 2008. The recession brutalized RV sales, so Forest River bought Coachman on the cheap. Some predicted Coachman quality would suffer since Forest River makes entry level RVs. However, Forest River was purchased in 2005 by Warren Buffett, of Berkshire Hathaway, who is well-known for demanding quality in his acquisitions.

My father, in his post-retirement job as a NASDAQ consultant, once visited Warren Buffett. He and my mother had purchased a forty-foot Bounder so they could travel the country while doing consulting. My father told me Mr. Buffett had a plain painted metal desk like the kind you used to see in public schools. That impressed me.

I found a more objective rating of RV brands in the *MOTORHOME Comparison Guide*, written and edited by Randall Eaton. The Guide performs ratings of manufacturers based on four categories: Construction, Customer Satisfaction, Dealer Rating and Resale Value. Each category has a possible of twenty-five points. The category scores are added together to create a total score. The total score ranks the manufacturers within their classification, Premium, Above Average and Economy.

The system seems subjective. On one of the web forums there was a comment, "It's only one guy." Eaton refers to having a team working with him: "…the author and research team are not responsible for actions taken based upon the content of this guide." There are no names of any team members in the Guide. Nonetheless, the Guide offers a plausible rating system and a detailed and informative description of many models.

I was anxious to see how Coachman came out. In 2006, Coachman was in the Above Average Class and was last of the six manufacturers in that class with 63 points and a rating of 5. The winner of that class, Winnebago-Itasca, had 92 points and a rating of 9. In 2008, the year Coachman was purchased by Forest River, it was placed in the Economy Class and came in fourth out of five manufacturers, just below Forest River itself, with 72 points and a rating of 6. For the next six years Coachman stayed in the middle of the pack. By 2017, Coachman had sunk to the bottom of the four manufacturers in Economy Class with 81 points and a comment, "Quality is suffering."

You meat-head!

Eaton writes of the Pursuit model, "Priced closer to a Class C, yet featuring many of the amenities found in a Class A."

The General Manager of Coachman responded, "We are very conscious of the economy and want to offer respectable products at a lower price point."

The main complaints from owners about the Coachman lines were that the factory and dealers were not responsive to customer's needs.

I called Coachman to get advice about upgrading my hitch receiver from a class III to a class IV so I could carry my Yamaha Smax and not worry about crowding the five-hundred-pound carrying capacity of the class III hitch. The receptionist forwarded me to the parts department where a recording instructed me to leave information.

The next day I got a call from the parts guy. I explained

my desire to upgrade my hitch. He, in a rote tone, recited that Coachman only recommended Ford-approved hitches be installed on the Ford chassis. I told him I had called several Ford dealers and none could give me a recommendation for a class IV hitch for a Ford F-53 chassis. The parts guy babbled something which sounded like more bureaucratic script. I said, "Thanks for your reply," and hung up.

I don't want to judge unfairly, but my radar is up.

If you are thinking about buying an RV, it is easy to research vehicles and manufacturers on line. The various forums offer invaluable advice. There are many published buying guides like the *MOTORHOME Comparison Guide*. Buy one or two. Read them. Don't be a meat-head!

CHAPTER 23

CAN RVS EVER BE GREEN?

The image of a giant breadbox lumbering down a highway does not inspire thoughts of aerodynamic design or fuel efficiency. More wooly mammoth than gazelle.

One blogger, irritated at the testing of a hybrid Winnebago, had this to say:

There is no more perfect example of ass-backward super-consumerism than the American recreational vehicle better known as the RV. Averaging roughly 4-18 miles per gallon these behemoths of the road cater to the super-consuming spoiled tourist encouraged to exist and actually admired in this country.

I have to admit, I formerly shared some of the irritable blogger's thoughts. I self-identified as a roamer of wilderness who treaded lightly upon the land. In my younger days, I backpacked and climbed mountains. I preferred back-country skiing on skins instead of the glitter of ski resorts. When I traveled around America in my old blue Volkswagen, I made do with a tent and a sleeping bag.

I don't know how old the irritable blogger is or if he tries to share time with a family. As the effects of age and a stressful occupation accumulated, I found it harder and harder to do the intrepid weekend-warrior thing. I still backpack and sleep under the stars in a bivy sack, but it's been a while since I climbed Mount Rainier or skinned up Mount Adams.

For my family, the RV was a way to travel in comfort. If we had travelled to Port Hardy on Vancouver Island in a car and had to stay in a tent or motels during the frequent rains, we would have been miserable. We could not have hauled home in a tightly packed automobile, the two four-foot long coolers of tasty salmon and halibut we had caught.

At this age, I will trade idealism for comfort. I still have an anti-consumerist, leave-no-trace mindset and I still feel nausea when I hear a pundit gargle out there is no scientific evidence for global warming. I re-read Ed Abbey's Desert Solitaire when I need a lift. If Ed had lived longer, he might have enjoyed the travel-in-a-home experience.

Is it possible to design a workable hybrid or electric RV? There are problems.

I bought a Toyota Prius as a commuter car. My primary motivation was to spend less on gas for my daily twenty-eight-mile commute. Gas prices were still over three dollars per gallon then. Interesting Fact: the graph of historic gas prices mirrors the U.S. unemployment rate.

It took a while to get used to the traveling-egg exterior style of the Prius, but I adjusted by comparing it to the Jetson's flying car. I felt good, as a cheapskate, cutting my gas expense in half. A lower carbon footprint was a nice side benefit.

One day, a friend told me I wasn't saving the world from global warming because the energy cost of manufacturing the hybrid's battery was extremely high due to mining of rare earth elements. It's true, manufacturing hybrid batteries produces more greenhouse gas emissions, GHG, than the production of conventional car batteries, but this is offset by lower GHG over the lifetime of the hybrid vehicle from less gasoline consumption and energy conservation from regenerative braking. OK Scully, you can retire now.

RV owners are sensitive to gas prices due to the fact that every time an owner pays for a fill-up he feels like he just got dope-slammed into the pavement. On discussion boards there is a lot of interest in a hybrid RV. One guy attached a shell to the back of a Prius, but there's no bathroom and no TV. Freightliner made a hybrid RV chassis in 2008, called the ecoFRED, by putting an Eaton electric motor and lithium ion battery on a Front Engine Diesel (FRED) chassis. Winnebago built a prototype thirty-six-foot Adventurer on the ecoFRED chassis.

In 2009, Brad and Amy Herzog and their two sons took the hybrid Adventurer on a fifty-day test run out of Chicago. Brad and Amy had made a living being spokespersons for the RV lifestyle, including a blog on GoRVing.com. The Herzogs appeared in many newscasts around the country and authored a number of books, including over a dozen children's books, many of which were alphabet poem alliterations. The Herzogs gave the hybrid RV high marks and noted that it seemed very quiet. Oddly, they never measured their gas mileage to see if there was improvement over the diesel-only Adventurer's eight mpg.

The Herzogs were bright stars of a growing culture who forsake the 9-to-5, purchase an RV, and make a living out of exposition of the RV lifestyle. The Herzogs didn't have to purchase their RVs since Winnebago gave them a different model, every year, for promotional touring. The RVIA employed the Herzogs for sixteen years and named them the "National Explore America Family."

Then Brad Herzog did an odd thing considering he must have known the nature and political persuasion of his bread butterers. On June 8, 2016, he started a Kickstarter campaign for the publication of yet another alphabet children's book, only this one was named, *D is for Dump Trump: An Anti-Hate Alphabet*. A blogger, Greg Gerber, known for disliking big government and dope-smoking idiots on his RV Daily Report, published his reaction to the Kickstarter campaign. Twenty-four hours later, the

RVIA terminated the Herzog's longstanding contract. Perhaps some consolation is had for the Herzogs in seeing *D is for Dump Trump* rate four-and-a-half stars with sixty-five reviews on Amazon.

Hybrid cars achieve better efficiency in several ways: aerodynamic design to reduce drag, regenerative braking to conserve the lost momentum, the idle-off switch that turns the engine off when not needed, and power assist from the electric motor that allows use of a smaller, more fuel-efficient gas engine. Stop-and-go, low-speed driving is more efficient than continuous-speed highway travel, the domain of motorhomes. Our RVs are at a disadvantage in harvesting hybrid efficiency compared to commuter cars.

Winnebago did not proceed with factory production of the hybrid Adventurer 35Z and I can find no detailed reviews of its performance. While Brad Herzog was dumping Trump and the RVIA was dumping Herzog, Winnebago was dumping the hybrid approach.

The hybrid concept for motorhomes may be a high bid. Perhaps RVs could amp up to an electric drivetrain? Electric cars, in the industry, are called BEVs, Battery Electric Vehicles. Hybrid Electrics are HEVs. Plug-in Hybrids are PHEVs and Forward Utility Carnot Kinetics are…well, you know.

Comfort in America is the dream of freedom. A part of that dream is the daydream of technological advance: life will become easier and desires fulfilled with less effort, less sacrifice. After all, Elon Musk sprouts new ideas like radishes.

We found comfort in Moore's Law predicting the number of transistors in our integrated circuits would double every two years. Swanson's Law massaged us with a vision of ever cheaper solar energy production. Could electric car batteries now be generating a similar law of increasing energy per-unit mass or decreasing per-unit price?

The advantages of electric vehicles are lower fuel cost,

lower maintenance cost, zero tailpipe GHG pollution and uncertain future tax breaks. The disadvantages are lower mileage range than internal combustion gas engines, much longer charging times compared to gasoline fill-ups, higher purchase price, and the gorilla of expensive battery failure. According to Bill Wallace, Director of Global Battery Systems Engineering at General Motors, the battery of a Chevy Volt in a hot climate, like Phoenix, will last at least 10 years, 150,000 miles, and 6,000 cycles with savings of $11,000 versus a 25 mpg gas car.

The green-ness of electric cars is dependent upon the green-ness of the electricity that charges the battery. If you charge your electric BEV in Minneapolis, say on a trip to visit Prince's house, your zero-tailpipe emissions would be responsible for 300 grams of GHG per mile due to the coal-intensive power generation in Minnesota. If you charged your BEV in California, where you could visit both Frank Zappa's old house in the Hollywood Hills and the Grateful Dead's Ashbury House in San Francisco, your emissions from Cal's cleaner electricity would be only 100 grams of GHG per mile. Hybrids are cleaner, lower GHG, than electrics in most of the U.S. except California, the Southwest, the Pacific Northwest and Florida.

In 2011, MVP RV Inc., an RV manufacturer that had purchased a Fleetwood Plant after the 2008 economic collapse, displayed, at a trade show, an electric, zero-emissions RV, a Class C, named the E Tahoe, apparently with no objection from Chevrolet. They claimed a two-hundred-mile range per charge. Commenters on Greg Gerber's RV Daily Report (yes, the same Greg Gerber that exposed the Dump Trump children's book), pointed out that the E Tahoe had the same size battery as the Tesla Model S, which has an ideal range of 300 miles, therefore the range of the much heavier RV must be exaggerated. One math wiz calculated the range of the E Tahoe at 35 miles.

No one, not even Brad Herzog, took the E Tahoe out for a test drive. Herzog would have been an appropriate choice since there's no reason to calculate mpg in an electric vehicle. It all became moot once MVP went out of business after a pledge for a $310 million investment from a sweetheart Chinese investor didn't materialize. The Chinese government controls exports of investment fortunes tighter than a cookie.

So far, no one has manufactured a viable RV hybrid or electric, but there are other roads to green for the RV industry. The carbon footprint of an RV, as with any motorized vehicle, includes not only its expulsion of carbon from burning fuel, but also the carbon cost of manufacturing. This includes the mining and transportation of basic source elements like aluminum, iron, rubber, silicon and petroleum, and the manufacturing of the final materials. The toxic potential of components contributes to the glow or non-glow of green as does the recycling of materials and the end-of-life environmental impact.

Ecolabeling is ubiquitous. Call it ubi-ecolabeling. I can't stumble erratically through my local supermarket without bumping into hundreds of products that have green certifications of unknown veracity. I look at the produce bins and then turn slightly and see a replica of every vegetable in the organic section. They look the same. I go for the cheaper doppelganger.

In 2009, T.R. Arnold and Associates Inc., TRA, an inspector of quality management systems in Elkhart, Indiana, ground zero of most RV manufacturing, began certifying RV companies and their products using National Green Building Standards. TRA awards four possible Certifications, ranging from Emerald to Bronze. Several Coachman products qualified for Gold or Bronze, but my Pursuit model isn't on the list.

Manufacturers pay TRA for the process of certification, which brings up a familiar conundrum. If you are paying someone for a service you hope will reveal something positive about your product, what is the chance they will say something negative? This all seems familiar.

Now I remember. The institutions that issued mortgage-backed securities, full of high risk loans, paid Moody's and Standard-and-Poor's for their ratings. The ratings fooled investors causing a world-wide financial collapse. Remember? For RV buyers, the TRA certification process is transparent and more objective than that of the Wall Street remoras. Purchasing a highly-rated RV will not lead to global financial collapse.

Part of the TRA Certification examines indoor air quality. RVs are at risk of high levels of formaldehyde from glues and adhesives. The California Air Resources Board set limits for formaldehyde emissions from specific building materials. Since my RV doesn't have a TRA Certification, I must now wonder as I drive the roads if I am self-prepping for my coffin. Either that, or open the windows every once in a while. Oh bother.

To misquote Shakespeare, who is certifying the certifiers. The Federal Trade Commission (FTC) oversees the burgeoning ecolabel industry. The FTC issued a revised Green Guides in 2012. This Guide gives general and specific examples of deceptive labeling, stating, "Marketers must ensure that all reasonable interpretations of their claims are truthful, not misleading, and supported by a reasonable basis before they make the claims."

The guide discourages terms like eco-friendly or environmentally preferable. An entertaining example was that of a laser printer pictured in a bird's nest, balancing on a tree branch, surrounded by a dense green forest above words in green type: "Buy our printer. Make a change." Although the ad doesn't make specific claims, the image conveys the message that the laser printer has some sort of environmental benefit. The FTC rarely pursues legal action, but issues warning letters in response to complaints about deceptive labeling.

Two days ago, President Trump announced his executive decision to withdraw the United States from the Paris Climate Accord. Over a hundred major corporations rose in protest. Corporations, as a general rule, don't pursue altruism unless it is in their interest, in which case it's not altruism. Could it be these businesses have discovered the green revolution is profitable and saving the planet is a nice side benefit? If President Trump is destined to walk through a gate of water, doesn't he want it to be clean water?

What about a better gas engine? Since its invention over a century ago, inventors have sought a more efficient internal combustion engine. Free piston engines use crankless, opposed pistons that power a turbine with exhaust gases. These engines have fewer moving parts, can run on multi-fuels and run cooler with less formation of nitrogen oxides.

The Huttlin-Kugelmotor, designed by prolific inventor Herbert Huttlin, looks like an oversized bowling ball. Opposed, curved twin pistons drive the entire combustion chamber in a circle guided by ceramic balls traveling in sine wave channels. The Kugelmotor can generate electricity or mechanical power or run a compressor.

The Five-Stroke engine has a low-pressure cylinder that runs on exhaust gas from two high-pressure cylinders, thus conserving energy wasted in a conventional four-stroke. Capstone Turbine Corporation makes micro turbines for cogeneration. The company is investigating the use of these small turbines in hybrid vehicles. Hydrogen fuel cell technology....well, you know.

The dream of green for the RV owner is still only that. You can buy all the right materials with certified construction and minimize your formaldehyde inhalation, but you're still guzzling six times as much hydrocarbon and producing six times as much greenhouse gas as that Prius that just passed you. Yet, at the campground, the Prius owners will frump in their stinky, humid dome tent, while you sip bourbon and watch a movie while your wife cooks dinner, or vice versa if you're not a misogynist.

Most RV travelers would like their horseless carriages to be more fuel efficient, their systems to be more energy efficient, their exhaust to be less polluting and their construction materials to be less toxic and greener. Currently, hybrid and electric technologies are not sufficiently advanced to power our big rigs over long distances. We will have to drive our mechanical wooly mammoths with the risk of irritating self-righteous bloggers!

ABOUT THE AUTHOR

William J Wood Jr, also known as Bill, lives in Clackamas, Oregon except when he can flee south. His previous publications include *Mothertime* (Trafford, 2006) a medical thriller, *The Essays of William J Wood Jr* (KDP Publishing, 2010) and *You No Buy, You Make Me Sad, a Journal of Thailand and Cambodia* (KDP Publishing, 2012). His album, *Tacos and Bowling*, still lives on Amazon.

OTHER BOOKS BY WILLIAM J WOOD JR

MOTHERTIME Trafford Publishing (2006)
[Mothertime- William J. Wo#9724D](#)

THE ESSAYS OF WILLIAM J WOOD JR
Kindle eBook

YOU NO BUY, YOU MAKE ME SAD
Kindle eBook

TACOS AND BOWLING (Album, 2003)
[Amazon.com- Tacos and Bow#9724E](#)

www.ingramcontent.com/pod-product-compliance
Lightning Source LLC
Chambersburg PA
CBHW041611220426
43669CB00001B/2